CHURCH

WHAT TO DO WHEN EVERYONE IS LIKE YOU

CHURCH

WHAT TO DO WHEN EVERYONE IS LIKE YOU

Daynette Snead Perez, D.Min.

AVIVA
PUBLISHING
New York

DIASPRA, LLC
PO Box 220944, Charlotte NC 28222
www.diaspra.com

Aviva Publishing, Lake Placid, New York, 12946
www.avivapubs.com

AVIVA
PUBLISHING
New York

Cover Design by Jason D. McIntosh
Interior Design by Michelle VanGeest

Library of Congress Control Number: 2021914854
ISBN 978-1-63618-057-1

Printed in the United States of America

ENDORSEMENTS

Rev. Dr. Daynette Snead Perez captures a generational challenge and offers a solution that will change the way we see and live out church for many years to come! Biblically rooted, theologically reflective, and practical without equal, the author emphatically reminds us to endure the "inconvenience" of the incarnation of a relationship with everyone, not just those who are like us. In this season of recovery and repair for ourselves and our churches, this is essential reading. *CHURCH: What To Do When Everyone Is Like You* is encouraging, inspiring, and timely. My best read of the year!

Rev. Jeremy Bell, General Secretary
North American Baptist Fellowship

When I met the Reverend Dr. Daynette Snead Perez in 2018 to organize disaster response efforts in the wake of Hurricane Florence, I was astounded by the diverse skillsets and networks she possessed. From her intimate knowledge of real estate and construction to her ease with crossing cultural divides, she identified congregations and neighborhoods overlooked by the larger community response and then built diverse coalitions to support them. She epitomizes a lifelong learner who shares with others the wisdom she has gleaned from many different sectors with generosity and grace. When she writes that she "know[s] from experience what it takes to build relationships with people from different backgrounds and cultures," or describes her **Stranger to Neighbor Ministry™** as her "superpower," she speaks the truth. This book takes the reader on a journey toward the unity which Jesus modeled and for which he prayed in John 17. Through practical illustrations, biblical reflections, exercises, and testimony, Dr. Snead Perez challenges us to become participants in the motus Dei, the movement of God in the world, through which the triune God fashions us into a new people who cultivate friendships in unexpected places. And it is precisely in those unexpected places and faces that we encounter Jesus in the guise of a stranger. This journey will change us, if we let it.

D. Steven Porter, Th.D.
Coordinator of Global Missions
Cooperative Baptist Fellowship

Daynette Snead Perez has been used by God to bring diverse persons together and to lead intercultural communities of faith. She offers a rare perspective with reflective and practical exercises in this book. You will be challenged to broaden your comfort zone and moved to love others who are different from you.

Dr. Rick Jordan, President
Bible Teachers, Inc.

Here is a book that actually helps us tackle a task that must be done if we are to be true to our gospel. Here you will hear the voice of a barrier-breaker, telling her story and offering us seasoned counsel. Here are observations about church health, friendships, outreach, even helpful conversational tips, and questions to provoke insight into your own hang-ups and the worlds of others. Listen up! Daynette Snead Perez has something to say!

> J. Daniel Day, Pastor Emeritus
> First Baptist Church on Salisbury, Raleigh, NC

Jesus prayed "that they all may be one" yet most churches betray an obvious lack of oneness. Rather than "unity in the midst of diversity" most churches are homogeneous. Yet most Christians also desire "a more excellent way" that incarnates a coming together of "every tribe and nation." But we lack the knowledge and a plan to get there. Daynette Snead Perez provides the church with a much-needed guide for dismantling our homogeneity and creating a more biblical approach to community. She provides a strong scriptural foundation, relevant examples and practical exercises that any group of church leaders can use to be "born again" as a church that moves its orientation toward its community from "stranger to neighbor." I highly commend Daynette and this eminently helpful resource.

> Dr. Larry Hovis, Executive Coordinator
> Cooperative Baptist Fellowship of North Carolina

Progress towards a more diverse, equitable, inclusive and truly intercultural church will be an uncomfortable journey at times. Dr. Snead Perez' book helps ease the path. In *CHURCH: What To Do When Everyone Is Like You*, you will find practical tools to thoughtfully consider your relationships, analyze your community, and steps you might take to turn strangers into neighbors. Churches looking to embrace the calling of advocacy must do more than book studies. We must get outside the church and establish new relationships. This book helps you move beyond discussions and towards actions that can build a beloved community. By doing so, your church can serve as a powerful witness to our divided world. For those ready for the journey, Dr. Snead Perez will help lead the way.

> Stephen K. Reeves
> Director of Advocacy for the Cooperative Baptist Fellowship
> Executive Director of Fellowship Southwest

To every stranger who became my neighbor,
my friend, and my family.

TABLE OF CONTENTS

SCRIPTURE PASSAGES for TEACHING

FOREWORD

For too long, North America has been preoccupied with debates on race, ethnicity, and social class. Some represent valid voices, while others may simply be random noises. Amid all this, Daynette Snead Perez' book, *Church: What to Do When Everyone is Like You*, is timely. As an African American minister of the gospel who, in most occasions, finds herself as an outsider of cultural communities other than her own, the author understands how it feels to be a *stranger* in an environment that enthrones *sameness*. This book exposes the gravity of the consequences of both misunderstanding and neglecting the basic principles that promotes healthy cultural diversity without sacrificing uniqueness. The author writes from the *heart*, being conversant with issues related to racism and the church's crucial role in racial reconciliations. Far from presuming as an expert on theology of culture or biblical worldview about race relations, she offers practical insights about maintaining *cultural individuality* amid the pressure for embracing diversity. She also speaks from personal experience, drawing lessons from her own intercultural journey. The author's previous missionary work among the refugees from Myanmar who resettled in North Carolina provided her priceless opportunities to be immersed in an ethnic community outside her comfort zone. In this regard, the author writes as a practitioner, yet her work is not lacking of academic substance. In nine carefully selected chapters, she invites readers to *look* and *listen*, *learn* and *laugh*, and *live* and *love* with those outside their own ethnic and cultural spheres.

The book reflects the author's personal journey as she employs accessible categories: wilderness, forest, journey, direction, stranger, new ground, going further, barriers, and landscape. These are powerful metaphors that serve as a trajectory to building relationships with those from "different backgrounds and cultures." Readers will find the DIASPRA EGGS logo informative, identifying the communities that Christians ought to serve and interact with on a daily basis. Dr. Daynette Snead

Perez is a master of *intercultural imagination*, with the ability to intersect theory and praxis and interweave elements from biblical theology, cultural anthropology, and contextual missions. Her work offers creative building blocks on establishing meaningful intercultural relationships, no matter how difficult. Every chapter is easy to follow, and the journal exercises are undeniably compelling because the intent is participatory. Even those who wish to stay within their own affinity or ethnic group will find the activities enriching. This book provides readers an opportunity to become active participants and invites skeptics to become authentic intercultural pilgrims.

In her Introduction, the author aptly writes, "We begin imagining our God image as water responding to rocks dropped onto the surface. Our responses are the concentric circles, radiating out into the world in everything we do, who we are, and where we go. Our God image is not limited to the fixed attributes of ethnicity, gender, generation, or social class." Evidently, this book highlights the power of the gospel to bridge various cultures for Christ and facilitates the *transition* of "strangers" to "neighbors."

Terry Casiño, ThD, PhD
Chair, North America Diaspora Educators
Global Diaspora Network—Lausanne Movement
Professor of Missiology & Intercultural Studies
School of Divinity, Gardner-Webb University
Boiling Springs, North Carolina

Lord,
Awaken my heart.
Widen my view of discipleship.
Grow the outreach of this ministry.
For the sake of the gospel, disrupt my comfort.
Guide me to grow relationships with people who are not like me.
In the name of God the Father, Jesus Christ the Son of the Father,
and the Holy Spirit.
Amen!

———— ❧ ————

God created humanity in God's own image, in the divine image God created them, male and female God created them. God blessed them and said to them, "Be fertile and multiply; fill the earth and master it. Take charge of the fish of the sea, the birds of the sky, and everything crawling on the ground." Then God said, "I now give you all the plants on the earth that yield seeds and all the trees whose fruit produces its seeds within it. These will be your food. To all wildlife, to all the birds of the sky, and to everything crawling on the ground – to everything that breaths – I give all the green grasses for food." And that's what happened. God saw everything he had made: it was supremely good."

GENESIS 1:27-31 (CEB)

———— ❧ ————

Introduction

In small towns and large cities, sacred spaces strike poses on valuable real estate. Yet, many beloved communities remain impoverished to reach across cultural boundaries for Christ. Our ministries are commissioned to reach all people for the sake of the gospel. However, many still remain isolated behind the walls of the church with those who only share in their sameness.

I know from experience what it takes to build relationships with people from different backgrounds and cultures. To begin this new direction in your ministry, to open doors for the departure of sameness and the arrival of cultural inclusivity, it is important to start from where you are now and redefine the church body in unity. Let's begin in the comfort of knowing we are all created in God's own image.

John 1:1 reads, "In the beginning was the Word, and the Word was with God, and the Word was God." Miguel A. De La Torre, broadens our understanding of the text through another cultural translation stating, the same text in Spanish reads, "En el principio era el Verbo." The English translates to, "In the beginning was the Verb." The difference between the two texts changes "the word" to "el verbo: the verb." "The Word" presents us with a fixed God in the form of a noun. But, the Spanish translation identifies the Divine as the Verb, which shows action. Accordingly, our God image is not in fixed form, such as our physical bodies rather, it is experienced through our actions.[1]

The images of God portrayed in human form may help us connect to the Creator, but those inanimate pictures are not based on the Living God.

In Genesis, our God image in action is described with words such as create, multiply, fill, and take charge. We are the *motus Dei*, the movement of God in the world.[2] I envision the Body of Christ as action figures proclaiming the gospel, intentionally reaching across cultural boundaries for Christ and reconciling ourselves to others. We are standing at the intersection of who we have been and who we wish to be. Who will we become? Are we courageous? Can we face the unknown with grace and love and ready to begin the journey into the wilderness of **Stranger to Neighbor Ministry™**? I am honored to be your guide because this is my story and superpower.

We begin imagining our God image as water responding to rocks dropped onto the surface. Our responses are the concentric circles radiating out into the world in everything we do, who we are, and where we go. Our God image is not limited to the fixed attributes of ethnicity, gender, generation, or social class. It is visible through our actions that reflect the Father and is already present in each of us. Being the image of God is revealed in relationships with strangers and neighbors alike. Each encounter is an opportunity to love, unconditionally — without judgment, restriction, or bias.

Paul defines our image as "baptized into Christ Jesus… heirs according to the promise," and proclaims the boundaries that separate us in humanity are all irrelevant. He goes on to state our actions towards others should not be divisive but rather encourage unity.[3]

Unity is the intentional action and continues to challenge how we gather as the Body of Christ inside the walls of our churches. We are commissioned as the salt of the earth, to enhance the world, to be lights shining in the darkness, and to serve by bringing strangers and neighbors into relationship with God. It is the pathway for discipleship, and the right steps will deliver us to new places with new people.[4]

But, the clock is ticking for our ministries and overshadows how we have learned to engage with others and gather as the Body of Christ. Systemic exclusion is visible inside sanctuaries on pews that confess who we are and are not reaching. Many of us remain mired in comfort with outreach limited to those who share sameness of ethnicity, gender, generation, and social class. *It's time to disrupt our comfort.*

We will focus our attention on the model of Jesus Christ, who often appeared as a stranger, but never met one.

This journey is for every ministry you build from this day forward to challenge the ways you are opening and closing the doors of the church.

If applied intentionally, **Stranger to Neighbor Ministry™** will widen your discipleship outreach.

As you navigate the way, it is important to complete the **log your journey** and **Stranger to Neighbor Ministry™ challenges** at the end of each chapter. Take time to work through the questions and to reflect on your answers. In the process, you will discover which actions are keeping you in the same places with the same people, and which actions must change for exponential discipleship growth.

This book shares my experiences of building relationships with people from all walks of life including a congregation that self-identifies as Myanmar refugees, a disaster response ministry, a community of believers in Westray, Scotland, and other beloved congregations along the way. Often as the sole African American in the room, I welcomed roles to serve alongside gathered communities that were different from me and up against unspoken church cultures where sameness from the pulpit to the pew is the norm.[5]

We transitioned from strangers to neighbors, our relationships were intentional and grew not from sameness but from inside our differences and shared identity in Christ. I pray you discover what to do when everyone in your ministry context is like you. Join me as we offer God's grace in our love for Christ, navigate comfort amid differences, and discover how to be present and in relationship with a multiplicity of people. Pray continuously to catapult a passage out from homogeneity with a handsome reward: a mixed fellowship of Christ seekers who disrupt the behaviors that lead to ministries where sameness is commonplace. May we recognize our cultural differences as a new normal in the places we gather together. Welcome to the journey!

LOG YOUR JOURNEY

Log your **Stranger to Neighbor Ministry™** journey notes. The goal is to know how far you have come, where you are in the journey, and most importantly, help others to follow your lead.

- This is what I am thinking now...
- Who and what I am praying for...
- For the sake of the gospel, growing intercultural relationships in my life and ministry context means... (Log any details about who, what, where, when, or why)
- One BIG idea to continue my **Stranger to Neighbor Ministry™** journey is ...

FIRST STRANGER TO NEIGHBOR MINISTRY™ CHALLENGE

- What questions are you asking to grow relationships with people who are not like you?
  - To God
  - To Yourself
  - To the Congregation
  - To the Community
- Establish a small support group of two–five people to pray for you and assist you in collecting the information you will need to complete the challenges throughout your **Stranger to Neighbor Ministry™** journey.
- In the past, how have you supported the congregation and the community in relation to people who are not the same as you?

Journey Notes

Journey Notes

_____

_____

_____

_____

_____

_____

_____

_____

_____

_____

_____

_____

_____

_____

_____

_____

_____

_____

_____

_____

_____

_____

_____

_____

_____

_____

_____

_____

―――――∽―――――

A voice is crying out: "Clear the Lord's way in the desert! Make a level highway in the wilderness for our God!

Every valley will be raised up, and every mountain and hill will be flattened. Uneven ground will become level, and rough terrain a valley plain.

The Lord's glory will appear, and all humanity will see it together; The Lord's mouth has commanded it."

ISAIAH 40:3-5 (CEB)

―――――∽―――――

ONE

Into The Wilderness

"You're a stump puller."

The sound of those words fell on my ears like old bricks landing on hardened red clay. After all, my plan was to heal the world with voice and songs. I was conferred with two music degrees and four years of intensive vocal work. Even though my parents ran a successful landscaping and paving business, I had no vision of working the dirt, paving asphalt, or leveling concrete for driveways. In the quiet of our meeting, he went on to say that my journey in life would continue in places where there were no roads. I would pull up stumps along the way and smooth the path for others to follow.

A few weeks had passed since I'd graduated college. Unaware at the time, the prophetic words were spoken by a pastor and family friend. He chose to listen to my dreams and speak over me, to provide a prayer and a confirmation for how my life would bring honor to God through Jesus Christ, the one who came not to be served, but to serve.

Over the years, his words have given me permission to walk into the wilderness. Instead of well-marked roads leading me from where I was to precise locations, I found myself confronted with a forest of obstacles challenging the way. What I did not know then was this, he was right. The trees were thick and planted firmly in place by gatekeepers not interested in seeing a new, inclusive landscape.

Even so, I managed to cross barriers as the first African American child to attend Skipwith Elementary in Richmond, Virginia, and to be photographed for the Girl Scouts annual cookie season,[1] and the first African American person ordained by a beloved community in Eastern North Carolina. With equanimity, trees were cleared and stumps uprooted to leave a solid path. I look forward to the day when there are no barriers to remove.

My friend said, "When you serve through Christ it will mean so much more to those who will follow next." I also understood it meant the chances of full acceptance in certain areas would continue to be challenging, but not impossible.

It was on that day that I claimed the truth of God walking with me. Those fresh beginnings seem so long ago. Today, I continue to move forward from my experiences from both the pew and the pulpit. I will share stories that will point a way to serve those who stand on the platform to navigate the wilderness of intercultural ministry and those who sit in sanctuary seats who have and have not questioned why all their friends are like them. The journey starts here.

My spirit celebrated the new experience of worship with a congregation different from my own, but let me be clear: I transitioned from a place of discomfort. I was a stranger standing in new territory, and there was no one to guide me. This was the first day of the journey to walk into an unknown forest, thick with uncertainty as a trailblazer for my new church community. I began awkwardly and did not know what I did not know. All I knew was that this congregation was exactly who God had prepared me to serve.

Arriving to worship for the first time, I could hear voices speaking Hakha Chin, one of the languages of the Chin people of Myanmar, but I was living in Eastern North Carolina where the sun rises and sets in colors worthy of coffee-table picture books. Here the BBQ is vinegar-based, and the pleasure boat filled waterfront is always nearby. My small town of New Bern prides itself as North Carolina's first capital and the "birthplace of Pepsi."[2]

Later, when I began to serve the congregation as a recent seminary graduate and an associate pastor, I had no understanding of the Burmese refugee journey to our small Eastern North Carolina town. The words of my Greek professor popped into my mind. He asked us to consider pastoring a local church because God had a big need to fill in small churches. I believed him because for the three years I served there I was filled with many experiences and again what it meant to be the other.

Thoughts flooded my mind as we started walking through the trees together and as pastor and congregation who were so different from each other.

For me, Hakha Chin was a complicated dialect to hear and speak correctly. At first, my ears focused on words that literally translated to English. The first words I learned to speak were God, Jesus Christ, and Lord. With the urging and smiles of the pastor and Chin congregation, my vocabulary increased, and from there I began to understand worship songs during Sunday service. Eventually, I graduated from songs to leading the call and response. On preaching Sundays, my sermons were translated to Hakha Chin by our senior pastor. To get through this fresh terrain, we all served together.

My fondest memory became reciting the Lord's Prayer with the congregation. Each time, the melodic prayer evoked the same awe as the English-spoken words I had taken for granted over the years. The universal message resonates in every language. One Sunday morning, the congregation presented me with a new name, Dawtchin, which means "love the Chin people." As Pastor Dawtchin, the name embodied inclusion and was a rare and special gift that honored my role as a servant pastor.[3]

God provided a unique path to grow in community together. More common than not, new church leaders replace someone with tenure and history. This was not our situation. For ten years, only the senior pastor served the refugee congregation. This time, the beloved community boldly called a pastor who was culturally outside the Chin community by recognizing the stranger God had placed before them. The effects of this partnership blessed us in a multitude of ways. Which brings us to the question, how are churches filling pulpits in the nation today?

Some sacred communities call search committees solely comprised of members who are known and respected within the same church community, but there may be obstacles to avoid. In this group, the particular slate of members may be unfamiliar with the changes within the community-at-large and seeking to maintain a status quo. As a result, the one called aligns with human perceptions of sameness with the search committee, the congregation, or even the ministry team. This could include physical characteristics of ethnicity, gender, generation, or social class achievements, including a specific college, family affiliation, or pastoral legacy. These ministers come aboard within well-established communities, fulfilling a time-tested preference of the congregation. As a member of several search committees, I have witnessed firsthand the inner workings of churches seeking newness or seeking sameness.

Newness-focused congregations seek to discover how God is moving within their church and the community-at-large, aligning God's commission with their local demographic changes, and identifying needs within the larger community. These sacred communities may openly confess a willingness to share community with and call pastors who are inclusive of the community-at-large for unity in faith.

Sameness-focused congregations seek to maintain the existing structures of the church and time honored traditions. Specifically this could mean retaining the theology, worship format, or congregational demographics. Here, new people are welcomed in and engage in traditional practices through assimilation.

Whether your congregation is focused on newness, sameness, or a combination of the two, congregations seeking new pastoral leadership are encouraged to take a deep dive inward by seeking outside consultation. The right consultant can awaken the congregation to who and where God is calling the Body of Christ based on God's mission, their location, the demographics within the community-at-large, the needs within the communities served, and vision of ministry growth within the church. This method can be eye-opening because every congregation has blind spots from the comfort of their own church culture. Outside consultants widen the congregational lens to expand awareness beyond their perceived existing boundaries.[4]

Regardless of who is called, the route taken, or the similarities to the congregation, the new pastor's presence temporarily disrupts the existing community who already share common characteristics including the faith community itself and sanctuary. It is commonly understood the fully formed community and new pastor spend the first year moving their way through a new "forest."

When sameness of cultural demographics, ethnicity, gender, genera-tion, or social class is shared between the leadership and the congregation, comfort levels are easier to find. But here's the thing — we are also called to serve in places where we do not find this immediate belonging and community. It has become clear to me that if we serve only in comfort, we intentionally honor Christ only inside the lines where we know the territory, our comfort zones.

And there is the pew side to consider. We often attend the same church for years and as we grow in community together for spiritual formation, our comfort increases. We know the worship format. We have become accustomed to the monthly meetings, the mid-week services, and the annual excursions and events. We can almost participate with our eyes closed. Worship is beautiful and predictable. Church life is comfortable.

But imagine now another view of the place where God's people gather. Imagine we are called together to serve not only in the comfort of belonging but in the discomfort of difference.

God calls us to serve unapologetically in ways that are risky and difficult. We should serve with fresh ideas on the leading edge of min-istry, but also on what I call the bleeding edge of Christ. Serving on the bleeding edge of Christ is a new understanding that every act of service brings *honor to God* because of the blood of Jesus Christ, which was shed for you and me.

One song reminds us, there is no place the blood does not go.[5] The bleeding edge of Christ carries us into service from the inside of our sanctuaries, through the aisles, outside the doors into unfamiliar places with people we do not know.[6]

Your **Stranger to Neighbor Ministry™** journey begins where there is little to no cultural understanding on your part; therefore, you will survey new territory, choose a direction, go into the forest, cut down the trees, pull up the stumps, and travel down a new path of service.

Let's listen for that voice in the wilderness and make a path.

It's important to note that the word "race" is not used in this book to categorize people groups. Race is a social identifier constructed during times of colonialism. Unsupportable by science or biology, the concept of race was conceptualized to oppress and disaffirm one people group and to benefit another group for societal position, privilege and power.[7] However, overt and covert discrimination of people solely based on the construct of race exists as "racism." In this book, the word ethnicity is used to identify different people groups based solely on ethnic identity. If you engage in conversations about racism, share this fact to help dismantle non-truths. You can have a big impact on how people in your sphere authentically discuss issues of racism and ethnicity.

LOG YOUR JOURNEY

Log your **Stranger to Neighbor Ministry™** journey notes. The goal is to know how far you have come, where you are in the journey, and most importantly, help others to follow your lead.

- This is what I am thinking now…
- This is who and what I am praying for…
- For the sake of the gospel, growing intercultural relationships in my life and ministry context means… (log any details about who, what, where, when, or why)
- One BIG idea to continue my **Stranger to Neighbor Ministry™** journey is …

STRANGER TO NEIGHBOR MINISTRY™
5 FRIEND CHALLENGE

This challenge provides a quick view of who is part of your inner circle of friends, who you are comfortable growing relationships with, and most importantly who you have chosen to build close relationships with. This is a mountain top view of your relational skills. It's a great start to recognizing your personal story and comfort level in building relationships with persons who do and do not share in your cultural sameness.

- On a sheet of paper write down the first names of your five closest friends.
- Write a 1 next to each person who shares your same ethnicity.
- Write a 1 next to each person who shares your gender.
- Write a 1 next to each person who shares your generation.
- Write a 1 next to each person who shares your same social class (economic status).

- Write a 1 next to each person who shares your same marital status.

- Write a 1 next to each person who shares your same educational level.

- Write a 1 next to each person who shares your same level of physical ability.

- Add the numbers next to each name. Your numbers will range from 0–7.

- Add all the numbers together and write it here. _____.

- Your numbers will range from 0–35. This is your **5 Friend Challenge Score.**

- Chart your results here.

| 0 | 5 | 10 | 15 | 20 | 25 | 30 | 35 |

00–07 Most of your close relationships are culturally diverse and inclusive

08–14 Many of your close relationships are culturally diverse and inclusive

15–21 Half of your close relationships are cultural diverse, the other half are culturally the same as you

22–28 Many of your close relationships are culturally the same as you

29–35 Most to all of your close relationships are culturally the same as you

A lower 5 Friend Challenge Score demonstrates your comfort level and relationship building skills are more inclusive of others who are culturally different than you are.

A higher 5 Friend Challenge Score indicates your relational comfort zone is building relationships with people who are the same as you.

Log about this challenge and what you have learned about your own relationship-building skills and preferences.

Journey Notes

Journey Notes

"Now when the Human One comes in his majesty and all his angels are with him, he will sit on his majestic throne. All the nations will be gathered in front of him. He will separate them from each other, just as a shepherd separates the sheep from the goats. He will put the sheep on his right side. But the goats he will put on his left.

"'Then the king will say to those on his right, 'Come, you who will receive good things from my Father. Inherit the kingdom that was prepared for you before the world began. I was hungry and you gave me food to eat. I was thirsty and you gave me a drink. I was a stranger and you welcomed me. I was naked and you gave me clothes to wear. I was sick and you took care of me. I was in prison and you visited me.'

MATTHEW 25:31-36 (CEB)

TWO

Through The Forest

"All Are Welcome Here!" Drive by any church and you may see these words or something similar posted prominently to encourage you to step inside and join the community in worship. I have often wondered about the success of posting banners and billboards to connect to strangers. These communities may be relying on what businesses call a 2P policy: Put up a sign and Pray.

The real ministry of the church begins when we open our hearts. In fact, it does not matter how many signs we install on the church property. If we're not growing interpersonal relationships from the beginning, we're not building community with strangers.

Every ministry in and outside the church building does the work of Matthew 25. In both real and metaphorical ways, our ministries welcome people, quench thirsts, feed, clothe, heal, and free people from bondage. Obviously, all ministries require us to build community with real people not just to post signs. If we fail to do this, how can we fulfill God's mission together, the Great Commission?

When we think of any movie, book, or biblical story, the drama unfolds a new or existing relationship and it only takes two people to start a community. Communities seek to draw its members near to comfort, calmness, and livability. They shape and influence experiences and interactions. In essence, the stories communicate relationships in community.[1] Our stories are the same and built by the relationships we grow.

A Bible Short Story: John 24:13-24

Jesus was a great communicator. His conversations with **strangers and neighbors** alike often met them where they were so He could point them to God. For example, when He appeared as a stranger on the road to Emmaus, Jesus began the conversation with a quick question. He asked, "What were you talking about as you walk along?" They shared how the community of believers was shaken. Their answers revealed what was, what happened, and what used to be. They talked about how Jesus died on the cross and His body was missing. They were not remembering the promise of resurrection but were stuck in the desolation of the past. By their answers, Jesus learned that only the past was on their hearts.[2]

I encourage you now to leave the past behind and focus on the resurrection of your ministries for new life. To move forward you will need to do something different. The **Stranger to Neighbor Ministry™** difference is recognizing "the body" is missing from the banners and signs we display on the front lawn of the church building. Strangers do not experience the beloved community by driving by and reading our words. When we grow relationships with face-to-face discipleship, we are the body of Christ revealed.

Our ministries are failing from the old ways of growing relationships. We must go out to meet people where they are instead we are waiting for them to come to us because they have literally seen our sign. Relationship skillsets are often learned early in life and those good manners keep us comfortable with people we are accustomed to sharing the same spaces. Usually, these are people who share our ethnic, gender, generational, or social class cultures. When we stay stuck in our own demographics, we limit God's work through us.

Learning **what to do when everyone in church is not like you** requires us to become intentional in how we interact with others and to transition from building community in sameness to leading ministries that challenge our actions and convey a "Christ-Centered Rationale for Diversity, Equity & Inclusion."[3]

Cries for justice are ringing out because of failures to build relevant stranger to neighbor relationships. We can authentically engage with people experiencing injustice by connecting those systemic issues in our own lives. By examining these scenarios, answers for justice are not far behind. We build empathy for the oppressed and recognize *them* as *us* and not apart from us. *They* are no longer outside *our* understanding but become a part of *our* inclusive story. When we authentically engage with persons different from ourselves, solutions for change become visible and lead to action.

A Bible Short Story: Esther 4:1–8:17

These actions are played out again and again in the Book of Esther. Ironically, its characters are front and center while the real and present God remains hidden. By Chapter 4, tension escalates between the king's head official, Haman, and Mordecai, a Jew and close relative of the newest queen.

Because of ethnic differences, Haman incites fear within the king about "a certain group of people" who followed "different laws." The king is convinced and awards Haman with the lives of the people and all their possessions. From his place of comfort behind the palace walls, the king barks, "Do what you want with them."[4]

The lives of God's people are in jeopardy because of their cultural differences and belief in God. Mordecai's loud protests outside the palace walls are reported to Queen Esther, his cousin. As messages are sent back and forth between the two, ultimately he sends his cousin a cryptic warning. "If you don't speak up at this very important time, relief and rescue will appear for the Jews from another place, but you and your family will die. But who knows? Maybe it was for a moment like this that you came to be part of the royal family."[5]

As a result of her actions, a new edict was signed by the king. It empowered her people with legal authority to save themselves and fight off the potential slaughter. Her people were transformed from death to life as a result of Esther's relationship with the ruler.

The Esther text hits the nail on the head when it comes to the power of relationships for transformational change. **Stranger to Neighbor Ministry™** is the solution for creating new intercultural relationships in life for ministry and God's mission.

Five types of discipleship are found in the Esther text. As you discover each one, complete the challenges and reflect on what this means in the context of your ministry. Discuss these challenges with others in and outside your church community.

1. **Palace Wall Discipleship** is visible with ministries that gather and exist only inside the walls of the church's physical location. Primarily it benefits only those who are part of the same church community. Here is your challenge:

    •   Identify all ministry programs that gather only inside the walls of the church and property.
    •   Explore at least one way each ministry could gather outside of the church's property and within the community.
    •   Discuss with the ministry leadership how the new location could benefit your **Stranger to Neighbor Ministry™** for intercultural discipleship.

2. **King Discipleship** begins with an understanding that every decision by the congregation and its leaders affects the church and the community-at-large. Each decision can be perceived as authored by gatekeepers or bridge builders. To widen the church's outreach, listen to all the voices in and outside the church community. Here is your challenge:

    •   Identify the voices each ministry is listening to when decisions are made.
    •   Identify a decision which demonstrates different voices were speaking and the ministry was listening.

- Discuss with the ministry leadership how new voices could benefit your **Stranger to Neighbor Ministry™** for intercultural discipleship.

3. **Mordecai Discipleship** has its ear to the ground and is available to sound the alarm when plans lean too far to the left or right. This discipleship is close to the people on the outside of the congregation and can engage with those inside the church walls as well. In this discipleship all warnings are authentic because the view of the church includes the community-at-large. Here is your challenge:

- Identify the persons or group that calibrates the church to the community-at-large so that ministry programs continue to serve in real time.
- How is your church community advocating for others in the community-at-large?
- Discuss how particular ministries began and reflect on how they can remain to benefit your **Stranger to Neighbor Ministry™** for intercultural discipleship.

4. **Haman Discipleship** chooses to close the doors of the church to others who are not a part of its current cultural groups. It is heard in the voices of those wanting to maintain sameness in both ministry programs and existing cultures within the church. Here is your challenge:

- What ministries have remained serving the same group of people year after year?
- Discuss the reason for sameness with the ministry leadership or group.
- How can these groups breathe new life and engagement into your **Stranger to Neighbor Ministry™** for intercultural discipleship?

Esther Discipleship — New ministries may present opportunities outside the church's normal activities. This type of discipleship is willing to take a risk and do something new so that there is a change in the lives of the people it serves. **Stranger to Neighbor Ministry™** for intercultural discipleship encourages us to partner with others in thought, prayer, and dialogue. We don't have to begin every ministry as an expert, just begin! Here is your challenge:

- How is your church demonstrating this type of discipleship?
- What are the risks?
- Whose lives are being changed because of the new ministry offering(s)?

> *Nine of the most powerful words*
> *you will ever hear or speak are these:*
> *"Because of our relationship,*
> *my life has been transformed."*
>
> —Dr. Daynette Snead Perez

LOG YOUR JOURNEY

Log your **Stranger to Neighbor Ministry™** journey notes. The goal is to know how far you have come, where you are in the journey, and most importantly, help others to follow your lead.

- This is what I am thinking now...
- This is who and what I am praying for...
- For the sake of the gospel, growing intercultural relationships in my life and ministry context means... (log any details about who, what, where, when, or why)
- One BIG idea to continue my **Stranger to Neighbor Ministry™** journey is ...

STRANGER TO NEIGHBOR MINISTRY™ CHALLENGE

- Complete the "Two Critical Questions Every Pastor Must Ask."
- Journal what you have learned about your community in relation to this exercise.
- Journal what you have learned about your ministry in relation to this exercise.

•—————————————•

Two Critical Questions Every Pastor Must Ask

1. Why Did You Come To This Church?

By far, this is the most revealing question you can ask when someone visits your church for the first time or a new member makes the decision to partner their spiritual formation journey with the congregation.

As a new guest or the newest member, they are experiencing the church with fresh eyes. This perspective will shed light on many areas of your discipleship outreach. Most importantly, the information is shared from an outsider who has stepped inside the doors of the church. Responding to God's call, they are the fruit of your ministry.

This critical question reveals how your discipleship outreach is serving in real time. Maybe they arrive because of how you are serving a specific group of people. Maybe their answer is tied to how God's message is conveyed in the culture of the church, a generational offering such as, elder day care, or a recent move to the area. The answer provides valuable insight into how your church culture is changing one person at time and building new relationships.

- Keep in mind who is arriving to hear the gospel.
- What new attitudes, skills, and ideas are being added to the community of the church?
- What possibilities lie ahead for existing and new discipleship outreach?

2. Why Did You Leave This Church?

On the opposite end of the spectrum is someone who has decided to end their spiritual journey with the congregation.

This is an insider and someone who has actively engaged with the congregation, ministry leadership, and programs within the church community.

Based on their perspective, you can gain valuable information about what is and isn't going well. You will know firsthand how ministry programs have served them and where ministry gaps may exist. You will also discover if communications are well received from the church or if there are breakdowns in communications, or unmet expectations.

Regardless of their reasons for leaving the church, thank them for sharing. Their answers have the potential to bless your ministry. The congregation can expand the ministry with the answers from a fellow insider who has been a part of the church.

- Discuss Question 1 with 1% of the church, or at least 10 people, who recently joined the congregation.

- Discuss Question 2 with 1% of the church, or at least 10 people, who have chosen to leave the congregation.

Ask the questions, listen, pray to receive the words to grow the ministry of the church. Be prepared and, if needed, ask additional questions for clarification. Whether you agree or disagree with what you hear, the dialogue will spark the heart of Christ, who always asked questions. Find ways to plug this information into the outreach of the church to benefit the **Stranger to Neighbor Ministry™** journey.

Journey Notes

Journey Notes

"Therefore, as God's choice, holy and loved, put on compassion, kindness, humility, gentleness, and patience. Be tolerant with each other and, if someone has a complaint against anyone, forgive each other. As the Lord forgave you, so also forgive each other. And over all these things put on love, which is the perfect bond of unity. The peace of Christ must control your hearts — a peace into which you were called in one body. And be thankful people. The word of Christ must live in you richly. Teach and warn each other with all wisdom by singing psalms, hymns, and spiritual songs. Sing to God with gratitude in your hearts. Whatever you do, whether in speech or action, do it all in the name of the Lord Jesus and give thanks to God the Father through him."

COLOSSIANS 3:12-17 (CEB)

THREE

Love The Journey

One morning, my office manager handed me a box wrapped in beautiful paper and colorful ribbons. I couldn't help but laugh when I opened the gift. Inside the box was a statue of the number one. He was a trekkie, a Star Trek fan through and through, and always referred to me as Number 1.[1] I keep the statue on my desk to remind me of the changes we inspired in the lives of so many people in the community. Prior to seminary, I served hundreds of families to find their perfect home. Through my business, I invested in and developed properties along the way, as well.

In 2000, I relocated from my Virginia farm to a small waterfront town in Eastern North Carolina. As a fourth-generation entrepreneur, the desire to create and manage new opportunities and challenges is foundational to my DNA. When it comes to out-of-the-box ideas, my mind begins in research and moves through the phases like a fish takes to water.

One idea for development began with the purchase of an existing one-story 1950's-styled building to transform into a modern, a two-story eight unit residential and commercial building. At the time, it seemed like a massive undertaking in the beautiful historic center, which had not seen any new brick and mortar construction since the 1990's. When all was said and done, the vision was realized. To this day, the units are in full use with quaint shops and residences. It is a beautiful contribution to the historic waterfront town.

Another accomplishment occurred during the annual luncheon of the Craven 100 Alliance, a public-private partnership created to advance the economic interests in Craven County, North Carolina. Each year, the Jefferson Cup is presented to the person who submits the closest to correct prediction for the Dow Closing at the end of the year. The winner is always announced in the next year's meeting.

Typically, the luncheon is attended by business owners, government officials, and financial leaders in Eastern North Carolina. It is an opportunity to hear the economic plans for the coming year. In 2019, their investments yielded $8.5 million. As a joint venture group, it connects those interested in growing the county's economy.[2]

In January 2013, I attended and placed my prediction in the bowl. The following year, I was shocked to be the winner of the Dow Closing Closest to Correct Prediction. Out of the financial experts, bankers, business leaders, and full-time economic experts, I had predicted the number closest to the 2013 Dow Closing and won the silver cup for first place. My entrepreneurial skillset of managing a small real estate company brought me into an unexpected spotlight.

The silver cup reminds me to take on new challenges and be willing to step outside my comfort level. When the journey is successful and unexpected, it becomes an added feeling of accomplishment.

There will be many firsts in your future as you grow relationships with people who are not the same as you. Scriptures point us in the right direction and identify who, how, and where to serve. Instead of the signs on the front lawns of our ministry, these verses are the first signs needed to identify to whom and how we build our outreach ministry. Just like Jesus, the Word points us to love God, neighbors, and strangers.

- *Love the Lord your God with all your heart, all your being, and all your strength. These words that I am commanding you today must always be on your minds. Deuteronomy 6:5-6 (CEB)*

- *You must Love your neighbor as yourself; I am the Lord. Leviticus 19:18B (CEB)*

- You shall treat the stranger who sojourns with you as a native among you, and you shall **love them as yourself**, for you were strangers in the land of Egypt: I am the Lord your God. *Leviticus 19:33-34. (ESV)*

- *Rather you will receive power when the Holy Spirit has come upon you, and you will be my witnesses in **Jerusalem, in all Judea and Samaria, and to the end of the earth.** Acts 1:8.*

The path of a **Stranger to Neighbor Ministry™** is where God calls us to focus our witnessing efforts.

In the diagram,[3] the first and smallest circle to share witness begins in our Jerusalem. Metaphorically, this is our first community and first caregivers. From this circle we learn how to communicate with family and non-family members and how to engage in appropriate social behaviors.

This is where we begin the process of building trust from caregivers to others outside our immediate family. No matter where we grow up or with whom, our first relationship experiences begin here. Child experts confirm feelings of trust begin to form during the first eight months of life.[4] Trust is built from these early development experiences of feeling loved and cared for. We are first called to witness within our immediate family.

DIASPRA EGGS Logo identifies the communities we serve.

From our family, witnessing widens to include everyone who is a part of our Body of Christ. This circle is our Judea. They are insiders within reach of our first circle and share community with us. Because we share community, chances are high we share commonality in culture and other similarities, such as preferences in worship, for preaching styles and theology. As such, there are elements of comfort and trust within this group and we may engage with each other on a regular basis. Our Judea is easily within of our sphere of comfort.

From Jerusalem and Judea, relationships expand outward to the next largest circle, Samaria. This is the community-at-large surrounding the congregation. We experience more differences in this sphere including cultures that are different from our own. This is where we meet strangers with rules of their own for building relationships. In order to navigate these new connections, we rely on what we have learned in past experiences so that we can manage feelings of unfamiliarity.

From the community-at-large, Scripture calls us to expand our witness to the ends of the earth. This is everyone else, the strangers outside the community-at-large. We may connect with this group through ministry efforts like disaster response, mission trips, or virtual platforms.[5]

In this book, we focus on how to build new relationships specifically in Samaria, which is outside the doors of the sanctuary but within the community-at-large. This is the place we have immediate access and where newness begins to transition from strangers to neighbors.

Opportunities to meet people for the first time often begin in the community. As you recognize the new people who join with your ministry to grow their spiritual formation journey and fellowship with you, begin to re-imagine a shift within the congregational DNA.

With each new member you become a new body of Christ. Maintain awareness about this changing environment. Adjust your comfort to stand in a canoe, rather than on firm land. As you lead ministry, re-center yourself to grow beyond your current boundaries. Begin by balancing yourself here and now, instead of who and how you engaged persons in the past and where you sat in the comfort of your ministry with people who were like you. Lastly, listen for all the voices to speak their truth. It will strengthen your leadership and honor all the voices as well.

Ministry is dependent upon whether you are able to reach people outside the congregation, into the community-at-large. If you remain in the same places with the exact same congregation, eventually the ministry will cease to exist as the lives of the congregation change year after year. Ministry success means that you are reaching people who are reaching people for Christ. The ways in which you transition strangers to neighbors will determine future destinations for the ministry.

The best way to grow relationships is to understand the meaning of community and culture. Community is "a group of individuals who have learned how to communicate honestly with each other, whose relationships go deeper than their masks of composure, and who have developed some significant commitment to 'rejoice together, mourn together', and to 'delight in each other, make others' conditions our own."[6] Culture, on the other hand, refers to the ways we express ideas, theology, and behaviors including physical representations such as; food and clothing.[7]

As we begin to explore, our focus is seeking community with other ethnic, gender, generation, and social class cultures. There are other types including geographical (American, Southern, or Northside culture) or communities based on different denominations or cultural practices of traditional, contemporary, and blended worship styles, just to name a few. Culture is expressed in everyday places, like restaurants and colleges.

From birth, community grows our cultural experiences taught by family and based on those expressions. We may naturally gravitate to particular people because we share community and cultural sameness. It is no surprise to understand the ease of engaging in cultures where we find comfort and navigate our living.

LOG YOUR JOURNEY

Log your **Stranger to Neighbor Ministry™** journey notes. The goal is to know how far you have come, where you are in the journey, and most importantly, help others to follow your lead.

- This is what I am thinking now...
- This is who and what I am praying for...
- For the sake of the gospel, growing intercultural relationships in my life and ministry context means... (log any details about who, what, where, when, or why)
- One BIG idea to continue my **Stranger to Neighbor Ministry™** journey is …

STRANGER TO NEIGHBOR MINISTRY™ CHALLENGE

In your Jerusalem...	Identify three discipleship opportunities that are connected to your family.	Example: family meal time or a family celebration event
In your Judea...	Identify three discipleship opportunities that are connected to your church family.	Example: an existing faith partnership or a new discipleship class
In your Samaria...	Identify three discipleship opportunities that are connected to your community.	Example: a local advocacy group or a disaster response ministry
Ends of the Earth …	Identify three discipleship opportunities that are outside your community.	Example: a virtual international prayer group

- Choose a community and discipleship opportunity to begin this new journey.
- Use this information to build existing and new relationships for the sake of the gospel.

Journey Notes

Journey Notes

One day Jesus and his disciples boarded a boat. He said to them, "Let's cross over to the other side of the lake." So they set sail.

While they were sailing, he fell asleep. Gale-force winds swept down on the lake. The boat was filling up with water and they were in danger. So they went and woke Jesus, shouting, "Master, Master, we're going to drown! But he got up and gave orders to the wind and the violent waves. The storm died down and it was calm.

He said to his disciples, "Where is your faith"?

Filled with awe and wonder, they said to each other, "Who is this? He commands even the winds and the water, and they obey him!"

LUKE 8:22-25 (CEB)

FOUR

Choose A Direction

Long before **Stranger to Neighbor Ministry™** launched as an intercultural ministry, I prayed for church leaders who would begin a journey to reach across cultural boundaries for Christ. I prayed for congregations willing to experience a change in direction and to transform the ways in which they were building community and making disciples for Christ.

When we build our personal discipleship with inclusive actions, our church community grows through inclusive relationships. The opposite view is ignoring God's commandment by holding on to unspoken and hidden rules that continue to separate us. Can we change our actions for unity in Christ or appreciate the uniqueness of our differences? Yes, we can do both. Jesus calls us to cross over to the other side of cultural sameness for oneness with others. Even as we experience the winds and the waves of our differences, we must choose to maintain the direction of one faith and continue the journey.

Life begins within a community of one, our biological mother. From the warmth of the womb, the fetus perceives experiences of touch, sight, sound, taste, and smell. Once born, socialization begins and the relationship between mother and child expands from the sole caregiver to the immediate family, outward to the extended family, friends, neighbors, and to meeting strangers. The child is exposed to a new set of cultural rules and community with each new person and place.[1]

Similar to the womb, culture is both visible and hidden and communicates itself through our senses. It partners with us in physical spaces and items, through our customs, and with our behaviors in places we worship, work, and play.

Events in the community communicate blatant and subliminal messages of culture. In neighborhoods, workout gyms, and everyday gatherings, the lure of culture is often what pulls us into the room or pushes us out. When we recognize this, the veil of not knowing falls from our eyes and we can identify the inclusive or exclusive nature of the cultures we navigate in community. There is no escaping it.

If we think of culture as an iceberg, only a portion is visible and above the waterline. There is much more we are not aware of because it is below the waterline.[2]

Cultural preferences are experienced when:
- We express theology.
- We trust those within our cultural community.
- We establish values that are acceptable to our cultural community.
- We shape ways of living and interacting with others.
- We utilize a common language and dialect.
- We engage in behaviors that are specific to and accepted by our cultural community such as:
  - Formal and informal events like worship and celebrations.
  - Preferences for food, clothing, and music.
  - What we own, where we live, and the places we go.[3]

Culturally speaking, there are many best practices to remain open to the culture of others. For example, when we meet someone for the first time, no matter what is observed through your senses, allow the other person to organically self-identify and share personal information about their own cultures, including their ethnicity, gender, generation, or social class identity.

Another way to demonstrate inclusive behaviors is by not assuming someone's identity or asking personal questions which can be perceived as awkward or rude. Instead, invest your time so that you can move beyond your senses to grow the new relationship. This will prevent being perceived as someone who is engaging in unintentional messages of microaggression.[4]

You can avoid these negative interactions by eliminating personal questions and engaging in dialogue that is more general in nature and encourages an open conversation such as; "I would love to hear more about your story." Or, "We welcome you as a part of this ministry and look forward to getting to know you better."

For congregations that find comfort in limited cultural identities of sameness, how we come together can polarize who we are by what we do, including the ways in which we gather to worship. Components of biblical worship; praise, reverence in awe, celebration through prayer, expression of music and song, and reciting the Word of God, are reflected in our church culture.[5]

Your goal is to identify your cultural rules, challenge your comfort levels, and reach beyond the cultural norms of your family and church to grow new intercultural relationships.

When I served the congregation of First Chin Baptist Church, it was within a different ethnic community. There was much for me to learn to become a part of this community. For example, before I could speak a full sentence in the congregational language, I began my linguistic journey by adding single words for Lord, God, and Jesus Christ in Hakha Chin while praying from the pulpit. At first, it sounded wrong to my ears to mix both languages together in prayer. However, the congregation responded positively to the new way in which I was praying. It was a holy understanding that I was learning and willing to acknowledge God first and commit to understand how to speak the language in worship.

Stranger to Neighbor Ministry™ encourages church leaders, individuals in the congregation, and the organization as a whole to attain cultural competencies when reaching out to the broader community. One author identifies this as our ability "to notice, respect, appreciate, and celebrate individual differences" and serve God's mission.[6]

There are different ways to identify cultural interactions and the terms are often misidentified and misused to describe a congregation or the ministry as a whole.

- **Intracultural Relationships** are between people who share the same or similar culture.

- **Cross-cultural Relationships** are between people who have different cultures yet, when together only one person or group is sharing their culture. Consequently, this is a one-way cultural relationship of mutual respect for each other. Short mission trips are good examples of cross-cultural experiences. In cross-cultural ministry, we typically can identify a giver and a receiver.

- **Intercultural Relationships** are between people who are significantly different in their culture, actively share their culture with each other, and receive the culture of the other. Competency in intercultural relationships demonstrate that you are aware of and acknowledge the uniqueness of others, sensitive to cultural differences, and have the skills to dialogue with and listen to others.

- **Multicultural Relationships** identify a gathering of people from different cultures and often misidentified to describe a certain type of community. Today, when a church or ministry is described as multicultural, it implies a "hodgepodge community"[7] of cultural groups. There is little to no cultural awareness or sensitivity, between its members and the individuals within the community do not engage through their cultural lens. Years ago, the term "melting pot" was a common term that carried the same meaning. Both terms negate the uniqueness of the cultures present and for this reason, are not encouraged to describe a theology, church, or ministry. Instead, you can acknowledge the many who gather together by using words such as intercultural, unity or unified. These words identify a community that inclusively embraces cultural differences through their actions. This can mean anything from the taste of shared meals, the words spoken, what is seen and on display to, the different sounds heard in the community.

The DIASPRA eggs logo was created as a visual reminder of how the church can reach across cultural boundaries for Christ. The concentric circles represent the various communities and the acrostic E-G-G-S represents cultures of Ethnicity, Gender, Generation, and Social class. In a nutshell, or shall I say in an eggshell, the logo represents the most common cultures we experience when we meet a stranger. Here's how I explain the connection with the church.

Real eggs are broken in two ways. The first is by applying pressure on the outside. Pressure causes the egg shell to crack. When this happens it no longer protects the embryo on the inside. The broken shell causes the egg to lose its potential to grow and carry life. Instead of protecting life, it must be discarded or the egg used for another purpose. On the other hand, if the pressure comes from inside of the egg, there is new birth and growth.

Across the nation there are abandoned church buildings no longer welcoming people to live the gospel. These buildings once functioned as gathering places for a congregation. But now, the gathered have scattered and only the shell of the building is left behind.

What happened? Either the congregation was unable or unwilling to serve the needs of the church community or the community-at-large. When this happens the congregation turns to a different model, moves to a different location, or disbands.

If the congregation disbands, it is often the result of its inability to build new relationships in the community, especially if the community has experienced demographic changes. In post-pandemic times, survival will require beloved communities to move outside the walls of the church and intentionally reach out into the community around them.[8]

The unwillingness of a ministry's leadership to adjust to the changes occurring on the outside of the church building leads to the ultimate death of that ministry. When ministry responds to what is happening on the outside of the ministry, the way an egg responds to the warmth of an incubator, it can grow from the inside, expand its outreach, and continue to serve the church and community.

If a congregation is not willing to change the ways in which it builds relationships, its survival is limited. Without growing relationships, church outreach slips away as the community changes. In this case, the congregation no longer grows its discipleship from the inside and eventually is unable to sustain its ministry. The church closes its doors and the building is repurposed to serve as an event hall, restaurant, condominium, or, if not repurposed, it is left to decay.

Another trait of a dying church is when focus is limited solely on the current congregation. By expanding discipleship outside the walls of the church, the congregation continues to grow. In **Stranger to Neighbor Ministry™**, growth is intentionally building intercultural relationships within the community for the sake of the gospel.

LOG YOUR JOURNEY

Log your **Stranger to Neighbor Ministry™** journey notes. The goal is to know how far you have come, where you are in the journey, and most importantly, help others to follow your lead.

- This is what I am thinking now…
- This is who and what I am praying for…
- For the sake of the gospel, growing intercultural relationships in my life and ministry context means… (log any details about who, what, where, when, or why)
- One BIG idea to continue my **Stranger to Neighbor Ministry™** journey is …

STRANGER TO NEIGHBOR MINISTRY™ CHALLENGE

EGGS Incubator Survey

In regards to the cultural demographics of your church or ministry, complete the **EGGS Incubator Survey** to document who you are serving now and who is waiting to hear from you.[9]

Ethnicity Demographics

What are the Ethnic demographic percentages of the congregation?

Based on the last census, what are the Ethnic percentages of the community-at-large?

What are the Ethnic demographics in the church's leadership?
* Pastors (total number and ethnicity)
* Deacons/Leadership Board (total number and ethnicity)
* Staff (total number and ethnicity)
* Laity Leadership (total number and ethnicity)

What are the Ethnic-specific activities that are offered by the church?
* Identify the ministry group and represent the ministries by individual count or as a percentage of the congregation.
* Determine the percentage of programs offered to the congregation based on Ethnicity.
  Example: English as a Second Language (ESL) Ministry — 42 participants; 3% of the congregation

Gender Demographics

What are the Gender demographic percentages of the congregation?

Based on the last census, what are the Gender percentages of the community-at-large?

What are the Gender demographics of the church's leadership?
- Pastors (total number and gender)
- Deacons/Leadership Board (total number and gender)
- Staff (total number and gender)
- Laity Leadership (total number and gender)

What are the Gender-specific activities that are offered by the church?
- Identify the ministry group and represent the ministries by individual count or as a percentage of the congregation.
- Determine the percentage of programs offered to the congregation based on Gender.
  Example: Men's Choir — 22 members; 29% of the congregation

Generational Demographic

What are the Generational demographic percentages of the congregation?

Based on the last census, what are the Generational percentages of the community-at-large?

What are the Generational demographics of the church's leadership?
- Pastors (total number and generation)
- Deacons/Leadership Board (total number and generation)
- Staff (total number and generation)
- Laity Leadership (total number and generation)

What are the Generational-specific activities that are offered by the church?
- Identify the ministry group and represent the ministries by individual count or as a percentage of the congregation.
- Determine the percentage of programs offered to the congregation based on Generation.

Example: Youth — Spiritual Formation Group and Youth Choir — 8% of the congregation
- Nursery
- Kids
- Youth
- Young adults
- Adults
  Ages 25-40
  Ages 41-75
- Seniors
  Ages 75+

Social Class (Economic Status) Demographics

To identify the income brackets (lower, middle, upper income) and percentages in your specific state, visit the Pew Research Center "Income Calculator."[10]

What are the Social Class/Economic Status demographic percentages of the congregation?

Based on the last census, what are the Social Class/Economic Status percentages of your community-at-large?

What are the Social Class/Economic Status demographics of the church's leadership?
- Pastors (total number and social class/economic status)
- Deacons/Leadership Board (total number and social class/economic status)
- Staff (total number and social class/economic status)
- Laity Leadership (total number and social class/economic status)

What are the Social Class/Economic Status-specific activities that are offered by the church?
- Identify the ministry group and represent the ministries by individual count or as a percentage of the congregation.

- Determine the percentage of programs offered to the congregation based on Social Class/Economic Status.
  Example: Youth — After school homework ministry with snack and food provided to feed the entire family for two meals during the weekend. — 8% of the congregation
  College scholarship ministry to high school graduates with financial need.
- Identify three next steps to build new opportunities for discipleship outreach.
- Share your thoughts with ministry leadership and begin a plan.

Based on what you have learned from the EGGS Incubator Survey....

What was most surprising about the cultural demographics within your ministry?

What cultural demographics within your community are missing inside the walls of your ministry?

How does this new information help you to grow ministry outreach across cultural lines of Ethnicity, Gender, Generation, or Social class?

Journey Notes

Journey Notes

———————— ❧ ————————

Jesus' disciples had forgotten to bring any bread, so they had only one loaf with them in the boat. He gave them strict orders: "Watch out and be on your guard for the yeast of the Pharisees as well as the yeast of Herod."

The disciples discussed this among themselves, "He said this because we have no bread."

Jesus knew what they were discussing and said, "Why are you talking about the fact that you don't have any bread; Don't you grasp what has happened? Don't you understand? Are you hearts so resistant to what God is doing? Don't you have eyes? Why can't you see? Don't you have ears? Why can't you hear? Don't you remember? When I broke five loaves of bread for those five thousand people, how many baskets full of leftovers did you gather?

They answered, "Twelve."

And when I broke seven loaves of bread for those four thousand people, how many baskets full of leftovers did you gather?"

They answered, "Seven."

Jesus said to them, "And you still don't understand?"

MARK 8:14-21 (CEB)

———————— ❧ ————————

FIVE

Encounter The Stranger

Stepping through church doors to gather with people who were not like me transformed how I see and hear the gospel. Worshipping with strangers became catalytic moments to engage in **Stranger to Neighbor Ministry™**. Specifically, what do you do when everyone in church is **not** like you?

Whether inside or outside of the sanctuary, every stranger encounter is an opportunity to recognize what God is doing and who we are seeing, how we are hearing, and actualizing the gospel through our interactions. In fact, our cultural lens shapes how we express our theology and ministry.[1] I came to discover that worship cultures can be polarizing acts of exclusion from the music (hymns, choirs, and praise teams) to words spoken (ancient to modern Bible translations), and to the worship formats (formal to informal).

Worship communicates the customs of the congregation and draws us into the sanctuary or not. Even as God's love embraces each of us, we seek and find Him through those human expressions. Every church engages in a unique worship, curated in culture to bring the congregation closer to God.[2] Yet, our human preferences separate us away from unity in faith.

For me, stepping away from worshipping only in my cultural sameness is what brought me to clearly see God's mission to all nations. I choose to worship in the company of strangers whether in the presence of high or low worship, the choir, the jeans-wearing pastor, or formal clergy attire. It is my relationship with God that connects me to worship Him. The language, the room, the music elevates the experience, but *my focus is God* and the privilege to worship in community with others.

Many times, I have interacted with congregations that did not share my traditions. My discipleship nature is not to remain distant but rather to encourage us both with a welcoming smile, or gesture, or even to share a brief conversation. Let's transition for a moment so we can answer this question: *What can we change so that our ministry grows new intercultural relationships for the sake of the gospel?*

Our cultures are initially taught to us by family members and past experiences. If we consciously think about our relationships and how they grew from the first meeting to the last time we talked, we may now be aware of how the relationship evolved, what happened, what went well, and what did not.

Based on how we perceive, speak, or experience the first meeting, every relationship encounters divergent paths, which direct us to stand still and keep the relationship in the same place, move forward and turn toward a closer friendship, or turn back around to end the relationship.

The journey begins with a stranger. The potential to grow this new relationship down the road is our decision to make. As we discover new opportunities to see, hear, and believe in our ability to grow intercultural connections, it is important to identify how relationships are formed and how our identity in Christ expands the relationship.

What is self-love in God?

*He taught them, "Hasn't it been written,
my house will be called a house of prayer for all nations?" — Jesus
Mark 11:17a (CEB)*

The first relationship to grow as we reach across cultural boundaries for Christ is to increase our understanding of God's love for each of us. A healthy relationship with our Creator means maintaining our prayer closet to listen for His guidance, speak, and pray our private thoughts, ideas, hopes, wishes, dreams, and feelings for only God to hear.

He is with us. God's trusted voice speaks to, through, and above us. Our physical, mental, spiritual, and emotional needs are ours to feed and care for in communion with Him. As houses of prayer, we exist to worship Him, to know the Son, and to experience the Holy Spirit in Love.[3]

Who is a stranger?

Early in the morning, Jesus stood on the shore,
but the disciples didn't realize it was Jesus.
John 21:4 (CEB)

Generally, a stranger is someone you meet for the first time. Stranger relationships begin and develop in public spaces like, grocery stores, sporting events, or even from the parking lot of the church. Strangers may acknowledge each other by engaging in eye contact and taking in the encounter including the physical appearance, dialect, mannerism of each other, and how each is responding, verbally, physically, and emotionally.

Conversations are limited to general subjects with little to no personal information shared between the two. Strangers may even choose to exchange information identified on a social media profile. When cultural sameness is not important, the two may perceive the conversation as relaxed, flowing easily with understanding. The exact opposite is likely to be true when cultural sameness is considered to be important and not shared between the two. It only takes a few seconds to perceive how well the two are interacting with each other. This interpretation sets up a sense of anxiety and uncertainty or happy anticipation for the second encounter.[4]

Who is a neighbor?

"The most important one is Israel, listen! Our God is the one Lord,
and you must love the Lord your God with all your heart,
with all your being, with all your mind, and with all your strength.
The second one is this, You will love your neighbor as yourself.
No other commandment is greater than these." — Jesus
Mark 12:29-31 (CEB)

In general terms, positive encounters with a stranger can lead to additional exchanges, moving the two into the next relationship level, a neighbor. This is someone you are getting to know, and the relationship develops around positive activities. Shared conversations are light and friendly and also held in public spaces. As comfort grows between the two, the conversation broadens to share positive thoughts and feelings, to discover common interests, but still little to no personal information is shared. This relationship is common in ministry. While timeframe varies, positive encounters with a neighbor can lead to the two developing a friend relationship.

Who is a friend?

"A friend loves at all times."
Proverbs 17:17 (CEB)

Friend relationships are primarily positive links between people who spend regular face-to-face time together. This relationship moves away from public spaces to trusting each other to meet privately. This is an emotionally supportive role. At this level, trust increasingly grows through sharing personal information and by reciprocating in supporting each other's needs. As a friend, we know the likes, dislikes, and character traits of the other. Friends are secure enough to express spontaneous emotions like laughing, teasing, personal stories, and life experiences with each other. This is a constructive relationship where positive and negative ideas can be discussed. No matter the subject, conversations between friends are more likely to wrap up in an upbeat way.

There is no timeframe to building a friendship; however, quality time spent together is key to growing a genuine connection with each other. In a church, community friendships are more likely to develop between members who share common positions or similar activities such as a spiritual formation class, a minister peer group, or a disaster response team. Consistent and positive encounters with friends can grow the relationship to the next level, a deep friendship.

What is a deep friendship?

"Don't urge me to abandon you, to turn back from following after you.
Wherever you go, I will go;
and wherever you stay, I will stay.
Your people will be my people,
and your God will be my God."
Ruth 1:16 (CEB)

A deep friendship is a trusted, long-term relationship that has been tested by experiences and survived the best and worst of times with a mutual commitment to each other. This is an important close relationship between individuals who seek advice and counseling from each other. Deep friendships are limited to relationships with people you would consider to be family, even if not part of your childhood household. Siblings, marriage partners, and long-standing relationships are common examples of people who share this level of connection.

Healthy relationships transition from God to self, to strangers, to neighbors, to friends, and deep friendships. Through each phase we grow escalating levels of trust. As you begin to reach out to new people, be encouraged to connect conversations with questions that are appropriate to the type of relationship.

Problems are likely to occur when you skip this organic development of friendships. It is awkward to have a friendship-like conversation with a stranger or a stranger-like conversation within a deep friendship. Be mindful of conversation that could potentially confuse the relationship stage and hinder trust.[5]

Ministry relationships with strangers begin through verbal and non-verbal communication. From your first face-to-face meeting to the last, be conscious of old influences from past relationships and experiences. Recognize the importance of developing trust and commonalities with people instead of tripping over your own cultural stumbling blocks that may prevent your light to shine. To become credible witnesses of the love and grace of God, keep your eyes open to all that the stranger communicates to you.

To encounter the stranger as Christ standing on the shore at the Sea of Galilee, is to move out of God's way so that our "we-ness" doesn't get in the way of our **witness.**

Strangers can appear when we least expect it, when we are engaged in our own activities like fishing in creeks, hunting for groceries, or worshipping in the pew. Regardless of what is happening in our own lives, a positive encounter with a stranger can be the "a-ha" moment to see and hear Christ calling out in a spoken word, a glance our way, or a gesture. If you listen and watch carefully, you may even hear His words to grow the discipleship of your ministry, "Have you caught anything yet?"

Lean in, engage, and recognize His presence is needed in you.

A Biblical Short Story: John 21:1–9

Jesus' crucifixion devastated His followers. They returned to the water's edge in hope of understanding Jesus's message, "But after I'm raised up, I will go before you to Galilee."[6] This was the same place He began his public ministry, walked on the water, calmed the storm, and fed thousands of people. The brothers Peter and Andrew, and John and James supported their families with long hours throwing, pulling, and catching their nets in the Sea of Galilee (Lake Tiberias). They were good at it and knew every detail of their hometown fishing hole, 13 miles long and 140 feet deep.[7]

For many days, seven of the Twelve waited there while the smell of dried, salted fish hung in the air and the water beckoned at their feet. On some days, the rough waters could challenge the handling of a 27-foot boat.[8] So, when Peter could no longer hold back the urges to feel the wet wind on his face, the others joined in, pushed the boat off the shore into the waiting freshwater, and jumped inside.

For one full day and one night the men navigated the vessel, relying on physical skills moving the heavy sails and nets. But the next morning, they had no fish to show for their efforts and good feelings were long gone. Instead of reliving the excitement of a large catch, they were dismayed by the emptiness of the boat. Even worse, they were unable to pay the taxes, harbor, and usage fees that would be required for putting their boat into the water.[9]

Heading back to shore, the men were hot from the sun, frustrated, and hungry. In this state of mind, they do not recognize the stranger on the shore who yells out, "Children, have you caught anything to eat?" Their truthful response prompted the stranger to add, "Cast your net on the right side of the boat and you will find some."[10]

When they did this, the net was almost breaking with fish of every kind. Looking back to the shore, this time with excitement, they recognized Him. The stranger now by the fire, offering food to feed them was the resurrected Christ.

Two weeks passed since they saw Him brutally beaten and crucified. I imagine if they had first recognized Him, they would have dropped their nets, jumped out of the boat, swam ashore, and rushed to embrace the risen Christ with thanksgiving to God. But this was not the welcoming party Jesus wanted.

In the midst of the old mindset and comfort of fishing, the men did not see the new God-given moment before them. Christ revealed, they dropped their old nets on the shore. Christ was now modeling a new relationship to bless their journey not as fishermen, but as fishers-of-men and women.

Surely, Jesus could have used another method to appear before them, but he had more to teach. With eyes to see and ears to hear, they added their catch to the coal-fired meal that was prepared for them and waiting.

As they listened to Him, Jesus transformed from an unrecognized stranger to the recognized Christ, from unloved to loved, from death to resurrection.

As we navigate land and water across cultural boundaries for Christ, we are also called to recognize Christ in strangers and to listen, to feed them at the edges of our own cultures, and to offer God's grace. I promise you, it will change your relationship with God and transform strangers to neighbors, to friends, and deep friendships. Are you ready?

LOG YOUR JOURNEY

Log your **Stranger to Neighbor Ministry™** journey notes. The goal is to know how far you have come, where you are in the journey, and most importantly, help others to follow your lead.

- This is what I am thinking now...
- This is who and what I am praying for...
- For the sake of the gospel, growing intercultural relationships in my life and ministry context means... (log any details about who, what, where, when, or why)
- One BIG idea to continue my **Stranger to Neighbor Ministry™** journey is ...

STRANGER TO NEIGHBOR MINISTRY™ CHALLENGE

1. Recall the last time you met someone for the first time.
   - Based on the information in this chapter, reflect on how, when, where, and why this relationship has evolved from the first meeting when you met as strangers. What was said, describe the place you met, write down the details of what you now recognize.
   - Is this person still a stranger, or do you now share a friendship, deep friendship, or something else? Why or why not?

2. Revisit your 5 Friend Challenge List.
   - Identify how you first met each friend as a stranger.
   - What shared event(s) helped to move the relationship towards becoming neighbors?

3. What shared common event(s) moved the relationship towards becoming friends?

4. For any deep friendships identified, how long have you known each other?

    •   Why do you consider this a deep friendship?

5. Reflect back on the EGGS (Ethnicity, Gender, Generation, and Social Class) cultures of each relationship.

    •   What can you now identify as your cultural comfort levels in building relationships?

    •   What can you identify now as a challenge to developing future relationships within other cultures?

Journey Notes

Journey Notes

Therefore, my brothers and sisters whom I love and miss, who are my joy and crown, stand firm in the Lord.

Loved ones, I urge Euodia and I urge Syntyche to come to an agreement in the Lord. Yes, and I'm also asking you, loyal friend, to help these woman who have struggled together with me in the ministry of the gospel, along with Clement and the rest of my coworkers whose names are in the scroll of life.

Be glad in the Lord always! Again I say, be glad! Let you gentleness show in your treatment of all people. The Lord is near. Don't be anxious about anything; rather, bring up all of your requests to God in your prayers and petitions, along with giving thanks. Then the peace of God that exceeds all understanding will keep you hearts and minds safe in Christ Jesus.

From now on, brothers and sisters, if anything is excellent and if anything is admirable, focus your thoughts on these things: all that is true, all that is holy, all that is just, all that is pure, all that is lovely, and all that is worthy of praise. Practice these things: whatever you learned, received, heard, or saw in us. The God of peace will be with you.

PHILIPPIANS 4:1-9 (CEB)

SIX

Breaking New Ground

It's one thing to read about the different types of relationships that are possible in your life and ministry. It's another thing all together to change the behaviors that will broaden your outreach. Reaching across cultural boundaries for Christ and moving beyond the relationships you have now will require you grow awareness and skills. So, where does this path lead?

Author Keith Broker says, "What is unconscious is not within a person's control but what is made conscious is available for human beings to understand, to change, or reinforce."[1] Bringing our attention to how we befriend new connections in the future will take us beyond our social media accounts. Let's first identify where we are and what needs to happen to build new relationship skillsets.

What to do when everyone in church is like you.

One major catalyst to grow intercultural relationships is recognizing that your friendships, ministry, and the members of the church are primarily with people who share your sameness. For many, the people in our relationship circles share the same ethnicity, gender, generation, or social class. Moving forward from here means changing how you are actually starting conversations and building relationships.

As a child navigating spaces with different cultures, I grew up experiencing difficult conversations from childhood, and it has extended well into my adult life. As a result, I enjoy friendships with people from all walks of life, from all over the world. We share different communities, so our relationships are rich in culture and full of grace.

While I was working on my master's degree, a seminary professor pushed me beyond the comfort zones of my worship activities.

At the beginning of a semester, one particular assignment challenged our cohort of pastors to broaden cultural experiences by worshipping with congregations outside our traditional denomination and to write about the experiences.

My first choice to complete the assignment and worship as a stranger was alongside a sacred community of Burmese refugees who gathered at a different time but at the same church location. I did not know anyone from the international congregation, and this one decision changed my life.

Long after the assignment was handed in, I worshiped with this congregation again and again. As time passed, we found community together. Eventually, the relationship grew from stranger to neighbor and then to congregation and pastor. It is a beautiful story of how God changes us when we least expect it.

I located another congregation, a small Greek Orthodox Church. Unable to connect with anyone prior to arriving, I took my chances and arrived early one Sunday morning and sat near the pulpit. It was a formal service spoken in several languages. I tried my best to follow along, singing quietly to ensure I would avoid any wrong notes. Unfamiliar with the setting, I was familiar with the God who provided space for me to worship in community.

After the service, several individuals introduced themselves and invited me to stay for the Sunday congregational meal. My first thought was to politely decline the invitation, but my heart won out. There was so much I did not know. I wanted to hear more about the flow of the worship and how the community came to gather in the small church. We spent several hours that morning exchanging conversation as fellow believers. The community was kind and welcomed me in.

Not knowing the unique worship of congregations that were so close by shrouded my view of God. This assignment opened my eyes, widened my lens of worship in community, and reinforced four stages to building intercultural relationships.[2]

I am not aware all my relationships are culturally like me.

The first stage is the ignorance of blind spots. This means you are not aware that all your activities are with people who are similar to your own cultures. Before the revelation of knowing occurs, you do not know that there are others who would welcome you into their lives. These others would grow your understanding of humanity. When you acknowledge your blind spots, you intentionally engage with more people who are not the same as you.

I am aware all my relationships are culturally like me, but I do not know how to change it.

The next stage occurs when you are aware your relationships are in sameness yet you do not have the skills needed to change how you are engaging with others. At this stage, it is impossible to move forward without more information. In essence, nothing has changed from the first stage except, you are now aware that something more is needed to grow your relationships.

Before I began serving at First Chin, I did not understand or speak the congregational language. My blind spot was not knowing how this new relationship would evolve, what questions to ask, how the dialect translates to English, or the process for learning the language. I moved forward by speaking to the senior pastor who became my language mentor. His willingness to share his position and privileges allowed me access to hear, speak, and write the native dialect of the congregation.

The same actions are required for church communities who want to build awareness and skills for new intercultural relationships. Blind spots are removed through education, listening, and engaging with people willing to provide and share first-hand knowledge of lived experiences. The way to grow intentional relationships is by spending time with new people in relationship and specifically by serving each other. Ultimately, new information will help you to understand what needs to happen next.

For example, a new ministry for women would require a conversation with the same demographic who have expressed a need for that particular ministry. Valuable information may be gained from the conversations alongside building new relationships. They begin growing relationships as they serve this specific population.

For another example, building a local skate park ministry would require a conversation with experienced skaters and local government officials to help determine needs and requirements to build the park.

Serving the community for social justice may involve engaging in activities such as book readings, conversations, and relational intercultural engagement. By learning from communities and groups who have experienced injustice and exclusion firsthand, participants are more likely to be awakened to existing issues and real solutions. The point is, when we recognize and remove our blind spots, our ministries can fulfill God's commission and address real human needs.

When it comes to growing a **Stranger to Neighbor Ministry™**, blind spots are eliminated by engaging with those you are seeking to grow in relationship with. Coming face-to-face with unknown challenges is likely to move you outside your comfort zones. Remember, as a listener you are choosing to hear firsthand knowledge so you can become aware that you do not know, what you do not know.

Consider these examples of blind spots.

- **Ethnic Blind Spots**: No awareness or skill to understand and dialogue on subjects like microaggressions, systemic position, privilege, and power, racism, and injustice.
- **Gender Blind Spots**: No awareness or skill developed to understanding gender self-identity and issues regarding pronouns, or the various needs within this demographic.
- **Generational Blind Spots**: Ministries experiencing issues because there is little to no awareness of building programs appropriate to generational interpretation, understanding, or needs.
- **Social Class Blind Spots**: Struggling to understand there are many socio-economic groups including varying degrees of wealth, middle-class, low income, and poverty.

Another example of when additional skills would be needed is when a ministry leader wants to begin spiritual formation classes to include members of a faith partnership, but without resources relevant to the cultural needs of the new members. Through her assessment, she becomes aware something is needed and begins the process of learning new skills by gathering the right information for a successful spiritual formation adventure.

Once she recognizes her blind spots and wants to continue, she becomes a learner. This means beginning with a study on her own, collecting resources, understanding cultural traditions, inviting a co-teacher in, or even taking a language course.

I am aware all or most my relationships are culturally the same as me and I am spending time and effort to grow new skills and intercultural relationships.

The third stage occurs when you are consciously aware of and actively engaging in the skills needed to reach across cultural boundaries for Christ. This takes effort. In this stage you are challenging your old habits and forming new ones. You are taking your behavior off automatic pilot.

Imagine learning to speak a new language. Your habit is speaking in your native tongue without consciously thinking about it.

If you're learning a new language, you must think about the dialect first and actually speak it when the opportunity arises. You begin with a few phrases you have memorized. As you consciously think about the words while speaking, using the phrase becomes a new habit.

Another example would be singing a praise song for the first time. You read the notes on the sheet music, but you have to think about the key changes in the song while singing on the platform. As you practice it again and again, the new skill becomes a habit. You eventually sing without the music. When it comes to forming new relationships, this could mean learning cultural traditions of an ethnic, gender, generation, or social class group so that elements for inclusive gatherings can be shared together.

Intercultural relationships exist in my life, ministry, and church, and I model Stranger to Neighbor Ministry™ with others.

In this final stage, you are aware of and actively engaging in the skills that are growing new relationships with people who are not the same as you. You no longer think about how you are crossing cultural boundaries for Christ, you're doing it! You can teach the skill at this level and enjoy authentic connections with people from different communities.

While I did not become fluent in Hakha Chin, we transitioned from that first meeting as strangers. Today, I can speak the Lord's Prayer in Hakha without first thinking about the English translation. The real testament to our relationship was the pastor who officiated my wedding. After twelve years of living in America, it was his first wedding ceremony in English and for a natural-born American. Inclusively, our prayers were spoken in Hakha Chin, of course!

Do I have it all figured out? No.

Am I making a difference in the *One Body of Christ*? Yes!

LOG YOUR JOURNEY

Log your **Stranger to Neighbor Ministry™** journey notes. The goal is to know how far you have come, where you are in the journey, and most importantly, help others to follow your lead.

- This is what I am thinking now...
- This is who and what I am praying for...
- For the sake of the gospel, growing intercultural relationships in my life and ministry context means... (log any details about who, what, where, when, or why)
- One BIG idea to continue my **Stranger to Neighbor Ministry™** journey is ...

STRANGER TO NEIGHBOR MINISTRY™ CHALLENGE

- Culturally speaking, are there blind spots you now recognize?
- What are your blindspots you can now identify?
- How does this information help you to navigate new conversations, relationships, awareness, and skills?

Journey Notes

Journey Notes

When they finished eating, Jesus asked Simon Peter, "Simon son of John, do you love me more than these?"

Simon replied, "Yes, Lord, you know I love you.

Jesus said to him, "Feed my lambs." Jesus asked a second time, "Simon son of John, do you love me?"

Simon replied, "Yes, Lord, you know I love you."

Jesus said to him, "Take care of my sheep." He asked a third time, "Simon son of John, do you love me?"

Peter was sad that Jesus asked him a third time, "Do you love me?" He replied, "Lord, you know everything; you know I love you."

Jesus said to him, "Feed my sheep. I assure you that when you were younger you tied your own belt and walked around wherever you wanted. When you grow old, you will stretch out your hands and another will tie your belt and lead you where you don't want to go. " He said this to show the kind of death by which Peter would glorify God. After saying this, Jesus said to Peter, "Follow me."

JOHN 21:15-19 (CEB)

SEVEN

Before You Go Further, Ask The Right Questions

Early one Sunday morning, I went into the sanctuary to prepare the platform with a visual cue for the afternoon message. The plan was to bring the congregation into the waterfront scene at the Sea of Tiberias by taping an outline of a boat on the carpet and placing a chair in the center of the invisible craft. The one-dimensional boat measured 27 feet long, 7 feet wide in the center, and reduced to a point at both ends. Its size roughly duplicated the measurements of the "Jesus Boat" discovered in 1986.[1]

The week before, I began teaching myself how to throw a fishing net purchased from an outdoor store. It took considerable time to practice the new skill, throwing it out and gathering it back in. Unfortunately, my efforts left much to the imagination, and the net continued to tangle. When it came down to the wire, my throwing skills seemed more appropriate for the children's sermon, rather than the adult congregation.

Fortunately, the senior pastor arrived earlier than usual and saw the net and the boat. Hoping for last-minute pointers, I asked if he knew how to throw the fishing net. He laughed and said, "All of us know how to throw this net." What I did not know was that within this church community were experts in fishing. My elated response was an audible sound of relief.

From my own cultural lens, I had not imagined my church family spent much time fishing the waters in Myanmar. It was without a doubt a teachable moment, almost missed. Several deacons flawlessly demonstrated how to throw the net into the carpeted waters. There was no matching the expertise, and what happened next became Plan B.

The voyage was now set with someone who had credibility. At the agreed time during the sermon, our fisherman would spring into action in front of the congregation. With smiles throughout the room and even a few hands covering faces, everyone listened for the message to unfold.

To this day, we remember the sanctuary fisherman and the sermon message encouraging us to break away from old habits that keep our nets empty of reaching others for Christ. When strangers appear before us, they encourage us to fish on the other side of our boat and to try new ways to catch others for Christ.

Not only did we see and hear the gospel that day, but there was also unexpected joy in our intercultural exchange. The answer came by asking the right question.

A Bible Short Story: John 21: 15–19

Jesus knew exactly the right question to ask Peter who denied the Lord three times over. This time the question about their relationship did not come from strangers in the public square, but in the company of trusted, deep friendships that had been tested time and time again. Sitting by the coal fire on the shore that morning, Jesus said the quiet thing out loud. "Simon son of John, do you love me more than these?"

The resurrected Christ wanted Peter to understand that love takes us outside our comfort and into places "where we don't want to go." Did Peter love Him more than fishing on the water and more than the other disciples? Did he love Him more than pulling in nets full of fish or the dangers of being a follower of Christ? Peter remembered how he feared for his own life and the words of denial he had spoken. Now, Jesus was there, and Peter confirmed his love by saying, "Yes."

Each time Peter answered, Jesus told him what to do by responding to Peter, "Feed my lambs," "Take care of my sheep," and "Feed my sheep." He wanted Peter to go, do, and be love. Jesus was still teaching the disciples that love is the mission.

I have served and prayed to fulfill this mission in spaces where my presence was questioned because of my ethnicity, gender, generation, or social class. In classrooms, businesses, and sanctuaries, these were some of the spaces that marked my story of **Stranger to Neighbor Ministry™**.

When I was 6 years old, my mother took my hand to register me for first grade in an all-white elementary school designated for our neighborhood. The principal met us in the office and after much discussion he told my mother school registration was closed, but another elementary school still had a few spots to fill. The other school was in another neighborhood where only African American children attended. My mother thanked him for his time, and we went home. After, my parents spent several days on the phone asking the right questions to an attorney and seeking legal advice.

A few days later, I was playing inside when I noticed a car stop in front of our home. A man slowly navigating a wheel chair from the back car door, carefully sat in the chair and began moving towards our home. It was the same man who had turned us away. On this day, he arrived to my front door to register me for first grade.

As the first and at the time the only African America student in the school, I was also the only child registered at the front door of their home. I entered the school to learn and built lasting relationships with classmates who welcomed me. Years later, my dad disclosed a haunting story. He told me on that first day, he drove past the school about thirty times worried about my safety and what it could mean to break through barriers in a town supported by systemic gatekeepers and Confederate monuments. My mother insisted this school would provide me with a good education. I am thankful for parents who saw my future as what it could be, unlimited and beyond their own experiences.

Later in life, I would follow in my parents' entrepreneurial footsteps and open my own businesses. I grew lasting relationships with strangers who I came to grow in relationship with as clients and in friendship.

The mission of love is the framework to grow relationships with God, ourselves, the church, and the community. The right questions engage conversations that can transform relationships and ultimately build trust. When we do this, we can change the stranger from unknown to known, unrecognized to recognized, and unloved to loved.

In 2018, when I served as a disaster response coordinator after Hurricane Florence, the journey meant bringing people together from different backgrounds and cultures. I gained lasting friendships with volunteers and those affected by the disaster.

One friendship began when a church decided to bring meals to residents affected by the high waters and my team was setting up the staging area for volunteers to arrive. As a church van drove up, a women peeked out to ask, "Would you like something to eat?" She went on to say that after learning of the damage, her congregation chose to provide hot meals, which were prepared and they were distributing in the small town. After our introductions, I learned she was also a pastor and wanted to know how else they could serve the community. The chance question from a stranger resulted in their disaster response team returning month after month to muck out, tear out, and rebuild homes. Today, this pastor and I have a deep friendship that began with a simple question.

When we ask the right questions and offer God's presence, we fill the gaps between the unknown and the known, which enables us to respond in equitable ways. One of the best ways to begin a conversation is by asking questions that encourage open conversations and are — Specific, Measurable, Attainable, Realistic, or Time-Specific.[2]

> **Specific**: A specific question is when you identify something in concrete terms for discussion.
> * What is one way you struggle to understand systemic injustice?
>
> **Measurable**: A question is measurable when the hearer understands the timeframe.
> * What goal do you want to accomplish this month?
>
> **Attainable**: An attainable question can be realized by the hearer.
> * Which relationships are you seeking to grow in your ministry this year?
>
> **Relevant**: A relevant question is important to the hearer and applies to their situation.

- Tell me about a time where your gender became the subject of a conversation?

Time-Specific: A time-specific question attaches end dates to the question.
- I would like to hear about your class schedule this semester, tell me about it?

The next step is to listen for the answers and engage in conversations that open the dialogue for positive interactions. When we do this, we sit where others sit and see what others see.

Just as Christ asked the right questions to Peter, we can follow His model to build a successful **Stranger to Neighbor Ministry™**. How are your current ministries serving to connect your congregation to your community-at-large? What questions are you asking to strengthen and grow relationships in all areas of your ministries and develop a consistent method to help your ministries stay on course? If you do not have a method of your own, start by using the **Stranger to Neighbor Ministry™** resource, **SMART Questionnaire.**

LOG YOUR JOURNEY

Log your **Stranger to Neighbor Ministry™** journey notes. The goal is to know how far you have come, where you are in the journey, and most importantly, help others to follow your lead.

- This is what I am thinking now...
- This is who and what I am praying for...
- For the sake of the gospel, growing intercultural relationships in my life and ministry context means... (log any details about who, what, where, when, or why)
- One BIG idea to continue my **Stranger to Neighbor Ministry™** journey is ...

STRANGER TO NEIGHBOR MINISTRY™ CHALLENGE

STEP 1: Stranger to Neighbor Ministry™ SMART Questionnaire

Prioritize the ministry goals in your church by keeping track of the progress in each ministry offered. This will instill a connection with the congregation, the overall church ministry, and remind the participants how the church community continues to question their ministry efforts.

Directions:
- Use the **Stranger to Neighbor Ministry™ SMART Questionnaire** or a resource of your own.
- After each meeting with staff, church members, and ministry groups, have someone rate the meeting based on each of the twelve questions.

STRANGER TO NEIGHBOR MINISTRY
SMART QUESTIONNAIRE

Rate your meeting from the following **ministry questions** on a scale of 0-5.

1. During the meeting, were participants connected to the overall mission of the church?
2. During the meeting, were prayer requests encouraged and prayer offered?
3. During the meeting, was the Word of God shared?
4. During the meeting, was community created and encouraged?
5. During the meeting, was the purpose of the ministry expressed verbally?
6. During the meeting, were opportunities provided for collaboration?
7. During the meeting, was active participation encouraged from everyone?
8. During the meeting, was biblical love demonstrated?
9. During the meeting, was spiritual formation growth achieved in some way?

10. During the meeting, were participants challenged to move outside their comfort zones?
11. Before or during the meeting, did participants engage in discipleship outreach?
12. Before the meeting, did participants invite strangers (guests) to the gathering?

STEP 2: Stranger to Neighbor Ministry™ Next-Level Questions

This next step is to help you move your SMART Questions to the next level by utilizing the questions of Jesus. Next-level questions will help you develop and evaluate your ministry meetings for growth and strengthen your stranger to neighbor commitment for God's mission and intercultural engagement.

- Match each SMART Question 0-5 scale rating to the **Stranger to Neighbor Ministry™ Next-Level Questions.**
- Answer any or all of the questions in the same level of the **Stranger to Neighbor Ministry™ Next-Level Questions.** Ask each ministry leader to maintain a Ministry Journal for the answers to the questions in the weeks, months, and year to come.
- Weekly and monthly leadership meetings are a great space to discuss and to pray for the challenges that are identified from the resources, **Stranger to Neighbor Ministry™ Smart Questionnaire** and **Next-Level Questions.**

If the rating level was Level 0-1 (Poor)	
Little to no awareness or skills developed in this area. Ask the following questions of Jesus to help you move to the next level.	
"Does this offend you?"	John 6:61
"What do you want?"	Matthew 20:21
"What are you looking for?"	John 1:38
"Who are you looking for?"	John 18:7

If the rating level was 2 (Fair)
You are now aware, but you do not know which skills are needed.
Ask the following questions of Jesus to discern possible answers.

"Do you want to get well?"	John 5:6
"How long has this been going on?"	Mark 9:21
"What do you want me to do for you?"	Matthew 20:32

If the rating level was 3 (Average).
Awareness is causing you to learn new skills.
Ask the following questions of Jesus to discover your thoughts on learning new skills for engagement.

"How is it that you don't know how to interpret the present time?"	Luke 12:56
"Do you believe this?"	John 11:26b
"Why are you sleeping?"	Luke 22:46

If the rating level was 4 (Good).
Good awareness and skills. You've formed a habit in this area.
Ask the following questions of Jesus to continue growing in your journey.

"What are you talking about as you walk along?"	Luke 24:17
"Salt is good; but if salt loses its saltiness, how will it become salty again?"	Mark 9:50
"Why do you fill your minds with these questions?"	Mark 5:22
"If they do this when the tree is green, what will happen when it is dry?"	Luke 23:31

If the rating level was 5 (Excellent). Excellent awareness and skills. Teach others what you know! Ask the following questions of Jesus to discover what more is possible.

"Do you see anything?"	Mark 8:23
"What are they like?"	Luke 7:31
"Do you believe I can do this?"	Matthew 9:28

STEP 3: DIASPRA EGGS Stages

The final step is to match each 0-5 level rating scale to the DIASPRA Egg Stages.

Rating Scale is 0-5. 1-poor, 2-fair, 3-average, 4-good, 5-excellent.

This step will help you to articulate each SMART Question for intercultural growth.

Level 1-2, EMBRYONIC STAGE:

These questions for your ministry are important to growing an intercultural ministry mindset. You are beginning to recognize this part of your ministry needs to be nurtured and fed.

To move to the next stage, continue to speak and hear the truth as you journey on. Identify the specific actions that will encourage the group to develop this goal as an important part of the overall ministry.

Level 3, EMERGING STAGE:

You are breaking the shell of sameness and emerging for new birth and growth.

To move to the next stage, consider seeking more opportunities to build intercultural relationships. Begin to connect with more people for the sake of the gospel. Stay the course and keep going

Level 4-5, EVOLVING STAGE:

Congratulations! You are leading in this area of **Stranger to Neighbor Ministry™**.

Continue to nurture inclusivity by listening to and reinvesting time, new awareness, and skills in your discipleship outreach. Continue to grow and re-evaluate the ministry on a regular basis. It's time to add a new version of this SMART Question to your list.

Journey Notes

Journey Notes

Jesus left that place and went into the region of Tyre. He didn't want anyone to know that he had entered a house, but he couldn't hide. In fact, a woman whose young daughter was possessed by an unclean spirit heard about him right away. She came and fell at his feet. The woman was Greek, Syrophonecian by birth. She begged Jesus to throw the demon out of her daughter. He responded, "The children have to be fed first. It isn't right to take the children's bread and toss it to the dogs."

But she answered, "Lord, even the dogs under the table eat the children's crumbs."

"Good answer!" He said. "Go on home. The demon has already left your daughter."

When she returned to her house, she found the child lying on the bed and the demon gone.

MARK 7:24-30 (CEB)

EIGHT

Remove The Barriers

Stranger to Neighbor Ministry™ has a No Church Left Behind Policy. This means, every congregation and church leader can find and start their journey here. As you grow cultural competency with new skills, attitudes, and knowledge, consider keeping an overall vision for what's ahead. Begin by re-imagining the future of leading a changing church and by maintaining the mountain top view. Meanwhile, keep listening to the feedback from all the relationships that speak into your ministry, God the head, the church as the hands and feet of Christ, and the community-at-large.

Sometimes, the rocky path is not seeing eye-to-eye with members in the congregation and a meeting of the minds is nowhere in sight. The best actions are to commit to the process, be willing to examine the issues together in a safe space, and to understand that these conflicts are opportunities to build relational capital.

Through it all, pray for resolution and honesty, move toward understanding and continuing to engage in equitable actions because, conflicts are normal community experiences.[1] But allow me to encourage you.

Your unique path will be unlike any other congregation's journey and when you encounter opposition, it may feel as if you're not moving forward. Expect that there will be delays and distractions. Let them encourage you that progress is being made and continue to work toward your ideal goal. As long as there is forward movement, you can avoid dead ends. So what could possibly happen?

Before the pandemic changed how we gathered as sacred communities, I was speaking with pastors and seminarians about how God was leading them to broaden intercultural engagement within their congregation. One minister mentioned how the community she was pastoring was excited to disciple new people who were not the same as the existing congregation.

However, after much conversation, she realized many did not want to change the ways in which the church worshipped together and shared community. As a matter of fact, they wanted new members to assimilate and become a part of what already existed. The plan was to remain the same, including to hold on to the existing worship formats and elements and long-standing annual programs.

For the newly hired minister this was unexpected, and she struggled to convey how the congregation could envision a new landscape to build new intercultural discipleship.

And there it was, the difficulty of re-framing conversations that have caused some churches to remain in homogeneity and stagnant sameness. Before we can move our congregations to accept, adapt, and integrate with oneness, we must move beyond how we deny, defend, and minimize our sameness.

This potential roadblock is known as the "FIG Complex." It is a combination of obstacles built with emotions of Fear, words of Ignorance, or feelings of Guilt. The purpose serves to generalize, demonize, trivialize, and identify other cultures as helpless or invisible.[2]

FEAR

As the congregation begins to broaden its intercultural outreach, the first barrier to jump over may be levels of verbal and non-verbal fear demonstrated by members of the congregation. Feelings of anxiety expressed and perceived may be anticipation of loss to the existing community. Some may be concerned with changes in church culture or other self-identifications of culture such as; the music or formal structures within the church.

It could be a financial concern such as hiring another pastor, or as small as adjusting meeting spaces. Regardless, these strong and unpleasant feelings are of great concern to the members and should be received and discussed in non-judgmental conversations. By providing active listening opportunities, you can engage members and convey to everyone that all their voices are valued and heard.[3]

How to fight fear:

*   Before engaging in large group conversations, gather small groups to discuss areas of concern. Smaller group discussions encourage intimate levels of communication and transparency.

*   Discuss the meaning of oneness in the Body of Christ identified in the scriptural text of Galatians 3:23-29.

*   When you recognize fear at the center of growing intercultural relationships, place God's word in the center by engaging in an interactive Bible study or preaching series with discussion. Utilize the texts below or other scriptures to address emotions of fear. (CEB)

> *"...whenever I am afraid, I put my trust in you —*
> *in God, whose word, I praise.*
> *I trust in God; I won't be afraid..."*
> *Psalm 56:3-4*

> *"Don't fear, because I am with you;*
> *don't be afraid, for I am your God.*
> *I will strengthen you, I will surely help you;*
> *I will hold you with my righteous strong hand."*
> *Isaiah 41:10*

> *"God didn't give us a spirit that is timid*
> *but one that is powerful, loving, and self-controlled."*
> *2 Timothy 1:7*

> *"There is no fear in love, but perfect love drives out fear,*
> *because fear expects punishment. The person who is afraid*

has not been made perfect in love. We love because God
first loved us. If anyone says, I love God, and hates a
brother or sister, he is a liar, because the person who doesn't
love a brother or sister who can be seen can't love God,
who can't be seen. This commandment we have from him:
Those who claim to love God ought to love
their brother and sister also."
1 John 4:18-21

• Prepare for intercultural newness now by developing a new worship ritual. When new members join the fellowship, celebrate in community by speaking a statement of faith in the form of an adaptation of 2 Corinthians 5:17. This sacred exercise will remind and prepare the gathered community that whenever new members join to grow their spiritual formation with the congregation, the church forms a "new" Body of Christ.

Original Scripture Text:

"So then, if anyone is in Christ, that person is
part of the new creation. The old things have gone away,
and look, new things have arrived!" (CEB)

Stranger to Neighbor Ministry™ Adaptation for New Community Confirmation:

(Name of New Member) is now a part of (Name of Church).
The old church has gone away, and look, new life has arrived!.
We have become a new Body of Christ.
We give thanks to God for (Name of New Member).
Together we will grow in our spiritual formation.
We are new in Jesus Christ, Amen!

IGNORANCE

As you seek to connect the church to the community-at-large, the second barrier may be from members who in their ignorance identify groups in general terms or speak inaccurately about people of specific cultural demographics.

Again, it could be a concern about how different areas of their personal church experience will be impacted, changed, or eliminated alltogether. With emotions and tensions high, it may be difficult to be on the receiving end of those conversations.

Be consciously aware of unexpected and blatant acts of ignorance. Racism, genderism, generationalism, and social classism are all conditions that thrive on the exclusion of others. There may be times the words you hear are not just from a lack of knowledge but rather a conscious ingrained unwillingness to honor the humanity of others.

In every space where the root of who we are begins with Christ, we are called to love others as ourselves, gather together, and form one body in a collective journey of His truths.

How to Fight Ignorance:

It is difficult to walk alongside people who refuse to honor the humanity in others and even more importantly who do not recognize themselves in the stranger. While it would be a great blessing to bring everyone on this new journey, this is not our burden. I encourage you to offer grace and understanding to all as you grow an inclusive future in intercultural ministry.

Never give up, but do what you can in your ministry with who you can. Focus on where God is moving the church and on the people willing to engage with strangers who do not share sameness of cultures. Sometimes the best action is to release and pray for the ones who do not share this vision. Release them to God and remain in His hope. We act for the sake of the gospel, to **go and reach disciples** and the Spirit of God moves with us.

1. The best way to fight ignorance is with the Truth.

2. Start an intercultural small group ministry. This will allow the group to build its own trusted community that offers support, encouragement, and acceptance.

3. Learn more about cultural exclusive terms including macro and microaggressions, privilege, and specific challenges faced by different EGGS cultural groups.

GUILT

The third barrier may include what Merriam-Webster identifies as "feelings of deserving blame especially for imagined offenses or from a sense of inadequacy." Recognition of living and worshiping in culture sameness may cause some members to feel guilty for not knowing the long-term existence and effects of "isms," systemic injustice, and discrimination.

For the first time, they may recognize their own experiences of living without the barriers experienced by other cultures. Awakened to the journey of others, what occurs next for some is awareness, empathy, and feelings of guilt for living without the emotional, physical, financial, or mental barriers faced by others.

How to Fight Guilt:

•   The **Stranger to Neighbor Ministry™** solution to fighting guilt is through knowledge. Consider utilizing one of the next two examples to gain additional information for congregational awareness. The first journey is an introspective one, **What is your story?**
    By discovering our past and present systemic stories in the four areas: basic, government, wealth, and media, we can gain a deeper understanding of how we have come face-to-face with, endured, or avoided systemic injustices.

Stranger to Neighbor Ministry Journey Chart

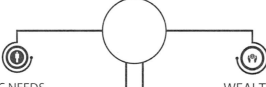

BASIC NEEDS

- Child & Family Services
parental care, healthcare, nutrition, childcare, foster care, adoption

- Education
zip code, public or private, elementary, middle, high school, undergraduate or graduate degree, scholarships, legacy grants, paid by _____

- Faith - affiliation & structure

- Healthcare - private, public, military

- Health & Wellness
access to medical care, mental health, trauma informed care, access to parks, recreation, exercise facilities

- Housing -
public or private, ownership or rental, rural, urban, suburban, type of loan (government, conventional, private) downpayment source _____

- Transportation - vehicle ownership, public transportation type

WEALTH

- Employment
job training, apprenticeship, trade school, formal education, business ownership, family business, job placement resulted from
_____

- Banking & Finance
business loan, grant, checking account, savings account, inheritance, stocks and bonds, investments

- Real Estate Ownership
residential, commercial, investment

- Insurance
healthcare, car, home, life, disability, renters

GOVERNMENT

- Social Security - retirement, disability
- Laws & Policies - local, state, federal
- Military - Housing, GI Bill,
Veterans Administration Loan, healthcare
- Criminal Justice System
municipal, state, federal

MEDIA

- Sports & Entertainment
childhood, teenage, college, adult
- Music
- Vacation
- Hobbies

- Your Basic Needs Story includes any information in areas of your personal family life, education, faith, healthcare, health and wellness, housing, and transportation history.

- Your Government Story includes areas where you have been affected, positively or negatively, by government agencies, laws, or systems such as; social security, local, state, and federal laws and policies, military, law enforcement, and the criminal justice system.

- Your Wealth Story includes areas of employment, banking and finance, real estate ownership, insurance, and financial history.

- Your Media Story includes areas of sports involvement, music, internet, vacation, hobbies, and entertainment.

• • •

TAKE SOME TIME TO READ THESE SHORT STORIES AND ANSWER THE QUESTIONS THAT FOLLOW.

Sean's Story
(basic needs, wealth, media)

Sean was an only child who lived with two parents in the suburbs of Raleigh, North Carolina. He attended public schools for eighteen years located near his same neighborhood. He joined the marching band and continued to grow his skill to play in wedding bands through undergrad. Sean graduated from a large North Carolina college paid for with a $20,000/year annual scholarship and a large legacy grant. After graduation, an alumnus hired him for his first job which led to meeting his now wife. Together, they attend the neighborhood church. His healthcare was provided by his parents and then by his employer. He and his wife own a three-bedroom/2-bath home in an area identified as increasing in value. The $25,000 downpayment for the home was a gift from their parents.

Sammy's Story
(basic needs, government, wealth, media)

Sammy grew up with three siblings. They were military brats. Before she turned 18, her family moved seven times and traveled all over the world. She speaks four languages fluently. Her mother died when Sammy was 20 years old. She attended the Naval Academy and after graduation, became an officer in the Navy. After eight years of military service, she transitioned to the corporate world where she enjoys managing a team of ten. Sammy is single, stays fit, and volunteers regularly as a translator for first generation immigrants. She attends a church where she often has the opportunity to speak several languages to people from other countries. She has a dog named Pilot.

Saylor's Story
(basic needs, wealth)

Saylor was a foster child. At 2 years of age, Saylor was adopted by a loving couple who were early baby boomers. Both parents were college professors. They were avid readers. Because both parents were professors at the university, Saylor enjoyed unlimited access to the library. When the economy downturned, neither parent had earned tenure and both lost their jobs. Unable to pay the mortgage, the bank foreclosed on their home, placing the family in a three-bedroom rental. They collected unemployment until the benefits expired. Several months later, one parent eventually found another job outside of teaching. Saylor moved out at 19 and became an apprentice for a local boutique grocery store. The owner knew her family well. Saylor also maintains a part-time job as a childcare provider during the summer months. Saylor's insurance is provided by the new employer and Saylor lives in a rental apartment with two other roommates.

Reflect on the 3 stories

- What do you identify as privileges in each of the three stories?
- What are the examples of someone receiving governmental assistance? Social capital assistance from acquaintances or friends? Are there any indications of generational wealth assistance?
- What are some of the benefits in their past? In their present? Are they linked?
- How did their past hinder their journey?
- When growing strangers to neighbors, how would understanding your own story help you to hear the story of others?

The second journey is seeking accurate knowledge of other cultures and communities, including its unique beauty and any challenges being faced. Educate yourself when you discover you have little to no awareness of a particular community, subject, or culture. Locate the right resources that will help you to understand the fullness of the community you are preparing to connect with and grow new relationships. Lastly, listen to the stories of others so you are no longer navigating in ignorance or making wrong assumptions.

LOG YOUR JOURNEY

Log your **Stranger to Neighbor Ministry™** journey notes. The goal is to know how far you have come, where you are in the journey, and most importantly, help others to follow your lead.

- This is what I am thinking now…
- This is who and what I am praying for…
- For the sake of the gospel, growing intercultural relationships in my life and ministry context means… (log any details about who, what, where, when, or why)
- One BIG idea to continue my Stranger to Neighbor Ministry™ journey is …

STRANGER TO NEIGHBOR MINISTRY™ CHALLENGE

- Meet with your ministry team or small group to answer the questions for Sean, Sammy, and Saylor's stories.

- In the journey notes, complete the **Stranger to Neighbor My Story Journey Chart** for yourself. You may also want to repeat the exercise to include parents and grandparents for a generational view and provide a wider lens of your family's journey.

- Reconstruct the four areas of your story: basic, wealth, government, and media. After you complete the details of your story, connect your information to identify personal and family advantages and disadvantages. To help you begin, answer these questions.

- Ask other family members and friends to complete this challenge and share their story.

    - Tell us about your family
    - Where did you attend school?
    - What was your first job? How old were you?
    - What did you do after high school?
    - When did you start working as an adult?
    - Who shares your household now?
    - How do you manage your healthcare?
    - Where do you expect to be in one/three/five years?

Journey Notes

Journey Notes

"You are the salt of the earth. But if salt loses its saltiness, how will it become salty again? It's good for nothing except to be thrown away and trampled under people's feet. You are the light of the world. A city on top of a hill can't be hidden. Neither do people light a lamp and put it under a basket. Instead, they put it on top of a lamp stand, and it shines on all who are in the house.

In the same way, let your light shine before people, so they can see the good things you do and praise your Father who is in heaven.

MATTHEW 5:13-16

NINE

Live Your Ministry In A New Landscape

A Bible Short Story: Matthew 5:3-16

Sitting underneath a wide sky, the crowd leaned in and waited. Breaking the silence, He spoke words to breathe the *motus Dei*, the movement of God, in the world. His words were not new laws from man to gain position, privilege, and power, but were the guides to living in the Father, modeled by the Son.

Gathered below Him, his disciples listened and learned how their gifts of salt and light were not theirs to keep. Their mission was to shine and preserve the Word with thoughts and actions of God's inclusive, unconditional love to strangers and neighbors alike. I imagine it felt as if time stood still.

The unfolding of **Stranger to Neighbor Ministry™** confirmed my post-graduation meeting with the pastor and family friend. His message was that God was giving me something to do, and I did not stand still. The nudging has continued to follow along, up, and through, to live my life and ministry in new landscapes.

In 2014, four planes and a ferry brought me to the quaint village of Westray, Scotland to complete my Master of Divinity internship. It was my second stay in the distant North Island, the first being a mission trip several years earlier. This time, I arrived on my own to serve as an interim pastor. The community welcomed me with the keys to the church doors and with opened hearts and homes. For me, it was an "out of the box" opportunity to hear God's message in one-on-one moments over tea, during walks through ancient ruins, and while listening to the harmonious sounds of fiddlers gathered for impromptu concerts.

Near the end of my stay, the beloved congregation surprised me with a long-lasting gift, a lift on the Guinness World Record's shortest flight in the world. My adventure was a two-minute island hop from Westray to Papa Westray.[1] During my stay, relationships grew from conversations over meals, prayer groups in community, and the intentionality of transitioning from strangers to neighbors.

It was shortly after this experience that, I began serving with the members of First Chin back in the United States. This time, broadening my boundaries meant shifting my cultural proximity from Scotland to Myanmar, and narrowing my proximity from across the ocean and sea to down the street. By the time I entered the doors to this church, the congregation was already navigating a culture different from their own and would help me to do the same. The faithful community accepted my inexperience of uprooting a family to arrive on foreign soil and determined to navigate a new life. Still, they welcomed me in to preach God's word, to live the sanctity of standing barefoot in the pulpit and raise my hands in God's praise.

In 2018, Hurricane Florence blew through Eastern North Carolina, damaging or destroying 4,300 homes in the New Bern area. I was called to a unique intercultural ministry leading a disaster response effort in a low-lying area, a small rural community outside the city.

A swampy odor lingered in the air surrounding the neighborhood that had been enveloped by the high waters. Piles of furniture, housewares, and memories were trashed to the streets to prevent fast-growing mold spores from consuming more of the homes' walls and contents.

As soon as the waters receded, our teams arrived to assess the damages. Eighteen months later, after hundreds of volunteers arrived with donations of time and skill to help residents rebuild their lives, many intercultural relationships grew between the community and the volunteers. To this day, these friendships remain as a vibrant testimony to the mission of love in action.

Stranger to Neighbor Ministry™ serves the liminal space between sameness and oneness.

It holds us inside of the *motus Dei* and the teachings of Christ, fills the gaps between us, and travels on roads to justice and mercy.[2]

Let's go and create community with whomever is before us. The power of this Love carries us into service wherever we are. From inside the sanctuary, through the aisles, outside the doors, into places that are unfamiliar, standing with, listening, engaging, praying and witnessing our faith with strangers as neighbors. I pray we embrace the challenge to move away from cultural sameness to navigate a new, stumpless landscape. Keep going! Pull up the stumps! Fill the holes! Lay down a new surface and light the path for others to follow!

For the sake of the gospel, this is the call to move beyond ourselves. To search for, seek and find the One Body of Christ (Jeremiah 29:13) and know, what to do when everyone in church is like you.

HALLELUJAH! HALLELUJAH! AMEN.

LOG YOUR JOURNEY

Log your **Stranger to Neighbor Ministry™** journey notes. The goal is to know how far you have come, where you are in the journey, and most importantly, help others to follow your lead.

- This is what I am thinking now...
- This is who and what I am praying for...
- For the sake of the gospel, growing intercultural relationships in my life and ministry context means... (log any details about who, what, where, when, or why)
- One BIG idea to continue my Stranger to Neighbor Ministry™ journey is ...

FINAL STRANGER TO NEIGHBOR MINISTRY™ CHALLENGE

- What are the cultural gaps that exist in your ministry context?
- How can you fill these cultural gaps and grow new intercultural relationships that build trust?
- Who are you equipping to grow intercultural relationships for life and ministry?
- What questions are you asking to grow relationships with people who are not like you?
    To God
    To Yourself
    To the Congregation
    To the Community
- In the past, how have you supported the congregation and the community in relation to people who are not the same as you?

10 STRANGER TO NEIGHBOR MINISTRY™
Milestones

1. Be intentional and committed to grow relationships with people who are not the same as you. Widen your community boundaries with other EGGS cultures: Ethnicity, Gender, Generation, and Social Class.

2. Join communities where your EGGS cultures are a minority, not the majority.

3. Engage in awareness of relationships by sharing common goals in community with EGGS cultures that are not your own.

4. Build relational capital for new inclusive community with others.

5. Be action oriented to dialogue and engage with others who are not the same as you.

6. Identify all the groups where you are a member or share community. Discern all the EGGS cultures within the group(s). Begin actions for inclusivity of EGGS cultures by growing in relationships with others.

7. Invite other EGGS cultures to become a part of a group or community. For all members to experience success, everyone must have genuine interest in the group's purpose for being.

8. Find avenues to share time and energy with all the members within your community so that you are building authentic intercultural relationships.

9. Leave old habits of sameness behind including, sitting in and going to the same places.

10. Be responsible for your own growth in building intercultural relationships. Take the time to become aware of and build the necessary skills to reach across cultural boundaries for Christ.

Journey Notes

Journey Notes

WHAT'S NEXT?

To experience
Stranger To Neighbor Ministry™ Virtual Edition
with Dr. Daynette visit:

StrangerToNeighborMinstry.com

To accelerate and grow your outreach
and experience next-level discipleship through a
presentation, seminar, or workshop,
bring **Stranger to Neighbor Ministry™** LIVE
and Dr. Daynette to your church or conference.

Contact DIASPRA, LLC at: diaspra.com/contact-us

——————— MORE WAYS TO CONNECT ———————

Author Website .... drdaynette.com

Business Website ..... DIASPRA.com

Blog .... liveyourministry.com

Course Website .... StrangerToNeighborMinistry.com

Facebook .... https://facebook.com/DrDaynette

IG .... https://www.instagram.com/drdaynette/

LinkedIn .... https://www.linkedin.com/in/drdaynette

Twitter .... https://twitter.com/RevDrSneadPerez

ENDNOTES

Introduction
1   Miguel De La Torre, *Genesis, Belief: A Theological Commentary on the Bible* (Louisville: Westminster John Knox Press, 2011), 14.
2   Warrick Farah, "Motus Dei: Disciple-Making Movements and the Mission of God," *Global Missiology* 2, no. 17. (2020): www.globalmissiology.org.
3   Galatians 3:27-29 (Common English Bible Version).
4   Matthew 5:13-16 (CEB)
5   Janice Daynette Snead, "Kan In Don Nah (All Are Welcome Here): A Framework for Developing Intercultural Worship Practice at First Chin Baptist Church of New Bern, North Carolina." (Doctoral diss, Gardner-Webb University, 2019). 2-6.

Chapter One: Into the Wilderness
1   "The Girl Scout Difference," Girl Scouts of America, accessed November 6, 2020, https://www.girlscouts.org/en/about girl-scouts/the-girl-scout-difference.html.
   I was a Girl Scout from the ages of 8-18. I contacted Girl Scouts headquarters to confirm my claim as the first African American girl photographed for the annual cookie campaign and shared a copy of an original mint cookie box wrapper. The photo was taken when I was an official Girl Scout Cadette. The representative could not confirm or deny my claim, stated there was no record of the photograph, and was not a part of the current archives until they received the copy of the photograph.
2   Snead, 3.
3   Ibid., 5.
4   "Ministerial Transitions," Cooperative Baptist Fellowship of North Carolina, accessed February 24, 2021, https://cbfnc.org/equip/ministerial-transitions-2/.
5   André Crouch, The Blood Will Never Loose It's Power, arr. by Nolan Williams, Jr, (Chicago: Manna Music, Inc; GIA Publications, 2001), 256.
6   "Called Together," a proclaimer message by Rev. Daynette Snead, Cooperative Baptist Fellowship North Carolina Annual Gathering, March 28, 2019.
7   Miguel A. De La Torre, *Reading the Bible from the Margins.* (Maryknoll, New York, Orbis Books, 2002), *24.*

Chapter Two: Through the Forest
1   William B. Gundykunst, Young Fun Kin, *Communicating with Strangers: An Approach to Intercultural Communication* (New York: McGraw-Hill, 2003), 340, 394-395.
2   Luke 24:13-25 (CEB).
3   "Diversity, Equity & Inclusion. *Christ-Centered Rationale for Diversity, Equity, and Inclusion." Witworth University, May 2016,* https://www.whitworth.edu/cms/administration/diversity-equity-and-inclusion/christ-centered-rationale/.
4   Esther 3:11b (CEB).
5   Esther 4:14 (CEB).

Chapter Three: Love the Journey
1   Angelica Jade Bastien, "A Beginner's Guide to the Star Track Universe," *Vulture.* September 25, 2017, https://www.vulture.com/2017/09/the-star-trek-universe-a-beginners-guide.html.
2   Craven 100 Alliance, https://cravencountync.gov/2089/About-Us.
3   Terry Casino, "Diaspora Missiology: When the Mission Field Comes to Us" (A Public Lecture Presented at Laidlaw College, Auckland, New Zealand, on May 23, 2017). https://vimeo.com/219665152.

4   Burton L. White, *The New First Three Years of Life: The Completely Revised and Updated Edition of the Parenting Classic* (New York: Simon and Schuster, 1995), 15.
5   Casino.
6   Scott M. Peck, Scott M.D., "The Different Drum: Community Making and Peace", (New York: Simon and Schuster, 1987), 59.
7   *Building Intercultural Competence for Ministers.* Committee on Cultural Diversity in the Church United States Conference of Catholic Bishops, (Washington DC : Conference of Catholic Bishops, 2014), 6-9.

Chapter Four: Choose a Direction

1   Jamie Morgan, MD. "Womb With A View: Sensory Development in Utero," UT Southwestern Medical Center, August 1, 2017, https://utswmed.org/medblog/sensory-development-utero/.
2   Peace Corps, *The Peace Corps Cross-Cultural Workbook: Culture Matters*, Washington DC. (U.S. Government Printing Office), https://files.peacecorps.gov/multimedia/pdf/library/T0087_culturematters.pdf.
3   Gundykunst, p. 88-89.
4   Capodilupo Wing, Torino, Bucceri, Holder, Nadal, Esquillin (2007) "Racial Microaggressions in Everyday Life.: Implications for Clinical Practice." *American Psychologist* 62,4, 271-286. https://sph.umn.edu/site/docs/hewg/microaggressions.pdf.
5   Snead, p. 51-57.
6   Fernando A. Ortiz, Gerald J. McGlone, "Model for Intercultural Competencies in Formation and Ministry: Awareness, Knowledge, Skills, and Sensitivity." *Seminary Journal* 16, no 2:24-30. EBSCOhost.
7   Terry Casino, Terry. Letter Daynette Snead to. Re: Proposed Project Titles from Daynette Snead. Email, 2018.
8   Thomas Rainer. *The Post Quarantine Church: Six Urgent Challenges + Opportunities That Will Determine the Future of Your Congregation. (Carol Stream, Illinois: Tyndale House Ministries, 2020), 103, Item 2, Kindle.*
9   Local, state, and national census information is available at: https://data.census.gov. Additional demographic information may be available through your local government (county, town, or city) websites.
10 Jesse Bennette, Richard Fry and Rakesh Kochhar. "Are you in the American middle class? Find out with our income calculator, *Pew Research Center,* July 23, 2020, https://www.pewresearch.org/fact-tank/2020/07/23/are-you-in-the-american-middle-class/.

Chapter Five: Encounter the Stranger

1   Jackson Wu. "The Influence of Culture on the Evolution of Mission Methods: Using CPMs as a Case Study." Global Missiology, 2014.
2   Constance M. Cherry. *The Worship Architect: A Blueprint for Designing Culturally Relevant and Biblically Faithful Services.* (Grand Rapids: Baker Publications, 2010).
3   Ephesians 5:29-30. *"No one hates his own body, but feeds it and takes care of it just like Christ does for the church because we are parts of his body."*
4   William B. Gundykunst and Young Yun Kim, *Communication with Strangers: An Approach to Intercultural Communication,* 2003, (New York: McGraw Hill Companies, 2003), 340.
5   Michael P McManmon, *"The 5 Stages of Friendship,"* Jessica Kinglsey Publishers, 2016, https://cipworldwide.org/2017site/wp-content/uploads/2016/02/The-Five-Stages-of-Friendships.pdf?x51364.
6   Mark 14:28c.

7   Nasa Earth Observatory, "Lake Tiberias (Sea of Galilee), Northern Israel," accessed November 20, 2020, https://earthobservatory.nasa.gov/images/40147/lake-tiberias-sea-of-galilee-northern-israel.
8   Madain Project, "Sea of Galilee Boat," accessed November 18, 2020, https://madain-project.com/boat_of_jesus.
9   Alicia J. Batten, Bible Odyssey, "Fishing Economy in the Sea of Galilee," https://www.bibleodyssey.org/en/places/related-articles/fishing-economy-in-the-sea-of-galilee.
10 John 21:5-6.

Chapter Six: Breaking New Ground
1   William B. Gundykunst, *Bridging Differences: Effective Intergroup Communication* (Thousand Oaks, CA:Sage Publications, 2004), 302.
2   Linda Adams, "Leaning a New Skill is Easier Said Than Done." Gordon Training International, accessed November 06, 2020, https://www.gordontraining.com/free-work-place-articles/learning-a-new-skill-is-easier-said-than-done/.

Chapter Seven: Before You Go Further, Ask the Right Questions
1   *"Jesus Boat — an ancient Galilee boat,"* Biblewalks.com, accessed January 12, 2021, https://www.biblewalks.com/jesusboat.
2   Doug Fike, Tony Stoltzfus, and revised by D. Lyn Eichmann. *Lifeforming Leadership Coaching: Professional Coach Training Manual* (Virginia Beach, VA: Lifeforming Leader-ship Coaching, 2008), 51.

Chapter Eight: Remove the Barriers
1   Gundykunst, 394-395.
2   USCCB, 23-24.
3   Gundykunst, 253-255.

Chapter Nine: Live Your Ministry In a New Landscape
1   Logan Air Scotland Airline. Orkney Inter Island Air Service Certificate. "This is to certify that Daynette Snead has flown on the World's Shortest Scheduled Air Service between the islands of Westray and Papa Westray as authenticated by Guinness World Records," May 9, 2014, Flight Number Log 361, Time Taken 2 minutes and signed by Captain Simpson, https://www.youtube.com/watch?v=zEezFUb8Zz4.
2   Micah 6:8.

ABOUT THE AUTHOR

*"Reaching across cultural boundaries is a ministry
to pursue with our hearts..."*

Dr. Daynette Snead Perez was born in Richmond, Virginia, and earned graduate degrees from both Regent (M.Div.) and Gardner-Webb (D.Min.) Universities. Equipping the church for unity in faith, she is a successful business owner, entrepreneur, author, and ordained minister.

During her years as a missionary pastor for First Chin Baptist Church, a Burmese refugee congregation in Eastern North Carolina, she learned a new language and reached across cultural boundaries like never before. The congregation also took her into their hearts and gave her the name Dawtchin, which translates to "love the Chin people."

After navigating waist high flood damage to her own home and, years later, severe area flooding from Hurricane Florence, her ministry shifted to coordinating long-term disaster recovery efforts with underserved communities in Eastern North Carolina.

Now, she is the Domestic Disaster Response Manager for Cooperative Baptist Fellowship, Decatur, Georgia. Her life's story makes great strides in areas that often present as barriers, even for churches.

Daynette and her husband live in Charlotte, North Carolina and — when she's not preparing for gray skies — she spends blue sky days cycling and running through gospel jazz tunes. She also writes a blog and guides ministries, places of worship, and seminary groups towards inclusive discipleship outreach and church growth through her ministry, DIASPRA.

Journey Notes

Journey Notes